THE SECRET MURDER
OF BRIAN JONES

RICHARD GILBRIDE

Printed in the United States of America

ISBN 979-8-89114-198-8 (sc)
ISBN 979-8-89114-199-5 (hc)
ISBN 979-8-89114-200-8 (e)

Library of Congress Preassigned Control Number: 2025911809

2025.08.22

MainSpring Books
5901 W. Century Blvd
Suite 750
Los Angeles, CA, US, 90045

www.mainspringbooks.com

IN MEMORY OF MY THREE LITTLE ONES

For nothing is secret that will not be revealed,
        nor anything hidden that will not be known and come to light.

Luke 8:17

CONTENTS

PREFACE

This book was inspired by a dream I had in the spring of 2020, and I still remember its vivid details several years later.

I was on a remote highway somewhere out West, a purple mountain range in the distance ahead, and behind me an undulating terrain that stretched into the prairie for miles upon miles. My old van had just broken down and there was no one in sight. I was the only human being in all of that desolate emptiness.

As I got out and assessed my unfortunate situation, I noticed a distant plume of brown dust, lit by the sun, approaching on the prairie highway. As it got closer I could make out the form of a white convertible, a sleek model from the 60s.

The driver had a blond moptop and as he slowed down and pulled up beside me, I could see that it was none other than Brian Jones.

"What's the trouble?" he asked. "I don't know," I said.

"Let's get it over to the side and have a look at it," he replied matter-of-factly, and he pulled up ahead to park his white convertible.

And then I woke up.

* * * * *

And so I began looking into who Brian Jones really was. I had grown up in the 60s, but I was more a Beatles fan than their bad-boy counterparts the Rolling Stones. I had seen them on the Ed Sullivan show a couple of Sunday evenings. Brian was the cool blond guy that played a sitar on *Paint It, Black*. I knew he had founded the band; his coolness gave them a distinctive mystique that set them over and above everybody but the Beatles.

What I had never realized was how mega-talented he was, what a musical genius he brought to the pop music culture. Brian Jones was a virtuoso with stringed instruments, keyboards, wind instruments, and he could also play percussion- a musician's musician, fluent in over 20 instruments. And he could play them quite well. And so many of the signature hooks in the Rolling Stones' pioneering and enthralling sound were due singlehandedly to his creativity and lifelong musical education. Yet he never seemed to get the credit he deserved, or any credit at all.

This book is intended as a case study of Brian Jones' death, which in my opinion, was absolutely 100% premeditated murder. This is essentially a criminological investigation. It is not meant to be a rock 'n roll historiography, although from time to time episodes will be recounted that pertain to the telling of the story. While researching his life and untimely death, I was struck by several particulars worth mentioning here.

Brian was of gifted intelligence, with an IQ of 135, and would aptly be described as a child prodigy. He was sight-reading music by age six. His mom taught piano and his dad played the organ and was choir director- which Brian joined at ten- for their Evangelical church, St. Mary's, in the holiday spa town of Cheltenham, England, about 80 miles west of London. By 17 he was also adept at clarinet, recorder, saxophone, harmonica and guitar, and he hitchhiked Scandinavia with his guitar the summer after completing his formal schooling.

His recklessness and promiscuity- he had already fathered two illegitimate children- culminated in parental scorn a few days before Christmas 1960. Brian brought his girlfriend home only to discover the house was locked, the electricity shut off, and a suitcase with his belongings was hidden behind a hedge in the driveway. The attached note explained that the family had gone to Wales for the holiday. For Brian this display of contempt cemented his break with his parents and the traditions of the British bourgeoisie. He knew on a deep subconscious level there could be no turning back from what he was grasping to achieve.

Brian Jones had a vision of electronic soul music, energizing the rhythm & blues of the Deep South in America and popularizing it for everyday English youth. And to this cultural tsunami he applied himself with a tenacity and focus described by a contemporary club musician as "streets ahead of us. He was very skilled musically, very impressive on guitar. We couldn't understand the chordal things he knew."[1]

By the time he founded the Rolling Stones in 1962, Brian was already a seasoned performer, having notched well over 100 solo gigs in the coffee bars and jazz clubs around Cheltenham. He customarily performed under the stage name Elmo Lewis, a takeoff on his given name- Lewis Brian Hopkins Jones- and Elmore James, a pioneering slide guitarist from the Deep South of the 50s. The same trailblazing mettle, hardened by his evangelical complexion and subsequent ostracization, impelled him to bring electric rhythm & blues to a mainstream audience. And thereby transform the pop culture of the 60s as profoundly as John Lennon, Bob Dylan, Jimi Hendrix and Jim Morrison.

Lennon and Jones were great friends and frequently hung out together in the late 60s. Brian contributed backing vocals and glasses clinking together on *Yellow Submarine*, and played an alto sax on *You Know My Name (Look Up the Number)*. They shared the same inner gestalt that would ruthlessly drive them to captain their fledgling rock 'n roll bands to the pinnacles of success in the post-Kennedy assassination counterculture.

Original bassist Bill Wyman explained that "Brian was the person that created the Rolling Stones in the beginning. He chose the music. He chose the name. He was the leader. He signed all the recording contracts, management contracts, all kinds of things."[2]

The club manager at the Marquee, which hosted their first-ever performance in 1962, recalled that "Brian Jones was the genius of the Stones. It was his extremely brilliant idea that they should be the opposite of the Beatles; that they should lurch on stage in street clothes, all leery. A deliberate marketing ploy."[3]

Lennon was extremely upset by Jones' sudden death. He was disgusted at the manner it happened- drowning in his own swimming pool- and remarked that it was "a terrible waste".

Dylan and Jones were also great friends and shared many impromptu jam sessions as well as LSD trips together. There was a period when Jones would telephone him on a daily basis. He would be buried in a magnificent

---

[1] Brian Jones: The Making of the Rolling Stones by Paul Trynka, Plume (2015), p. 45
[2] Interview of Bill Wyman by Lindsey Parker, Yahoo Music 2019
[3] Trynka, p. 79

silver and bronze casket flown in from the United States and paid for by Bob Dylan.

And Brian bonded even closer with another revolutionary rock icon from the 60s, Jimi Hendrix. He was in the audience for the inaugural 1966 London gig of the Jimi Hendrix Experience, and was influential in helping them use the Stones' Olympic Studios to record their first album. Brian was expressly asked to introduce Jimi at the 1967 Monterrey Pop Festival; the relative unknown seared his way into American awareness with a legendary guitar-burning spectacle. During Jones' decline, he drunkenly stumbled into a recording session of *All Along the Watchtower* and played a cacophonous piano before falling asleep in the studio. Jones contributed the vibraslap, a newly-invented percussion instrument, in the finished track of the song. Hendrix was puzzled by the cavalier manner in which the surviving Stones treated Jones' death.

Jim Morrison wrote a tribute poem a few days after the drowning, *Ode to L.A. While Thinking of Brian Jones, Deceased*. He printed up 500 copies and personally handed them out before a concert two weeks later at the Aquarius Theatre in Hollywood. It is more than notable that Morrison would die on July 3, 1971- exactly two years after Jones' officially-determined date of death.

Personally I learned about the death of Brian Jones as a 14-year-old youngster growing up in Boston. One sunny summer morning I was leafing through the *Boston Globe*, which our family subscribed to, and at the back of the first section noticed a one-paragraph blurb about the Stones' guitarist's accidental drowning. I was stunned. I realized he was the founder and leader of the Stones and I didn't understand how they could continue on as a rock band after losing such a key member. They were one of the few bands- the others being the Beatles, the Doors and the Monkees- that I knew the name of every member.

During a trip to Morocco for July into August of 1968, Jones preserved the exotic sounds of the local musicians for an album titled **Brian Jones Presents the Pipes of Pan at Jojouka**. They performed on rhaitas and tbel drums for their annual Rites of Pan festival, which Brian attended with his girlfriend at the time, Suki Potier. As they reclined on cushions observing the ritual ceremony, "the most beautiful goat anyone had ever seen" was led in front of them. It was snow-white, with a fringe of blond hair. Brian jumped up and shouted, "That's me!" And the goat was then taken off to be slaughtered.

It was not long afterward that his bandmate Keith Richards told him, "You'll never make it to thirty, man."

"I know," Jones said.

A few weeks before his death Brian had a reconciliation with his parents, inviting them over for dinner at his Cotchford Farm estate. Purchased the previous November, it had once belonged to A.A. Milne, the creator of the Winnie the Pooh books. The initiator of the Stones juggernaut was happy to have made a successful career in music- one which far exceeded the expectations of his middle-class parents.

"I could live here all my life," he told them.

And Brian Jones indeed did just that, although he didn't know his life would soon be cut short.

Cotchford Farm in Hartfield, East Sussex

ONE

THE BURN PILE

The body of Brian Jones was pulled from the swimming pool at Cotchford Farm officially around midnight on July 2, 1969- although this may have been as early as 9:30 PM. Incredibly, his body lay beside the pool until dawn broke on July 3rd.

Shortly after midnight, the first police officer arrived at the scene. PC Albert Evans had a 'policeman's instinct' that he wasn't being given the full story, but he had nothing tangible to justify his suspicions.[4] But these

---

[4] Trynka, p. 315

1

were immediately raised when the ambulance that had been dispatched to the scene, shortly before Evans, drove away without the body.

As Evans would recall, decades later, "After the local doctor had pronounced Brian Jones dead, the ambulance men and the doctor left without the body. I stayed with the body all night and then accompanied it around dawn, to the East Grinstead Hospital where I saw it placed into a cold storage compartment by a mortuary assistant." [5]

The ambulance had instead taken Frank Thorogood to the hospital for treatment for a badly injured wrist. Thorogood was a builder who'd moved into a garage apartment at Cotchford only a few days after Jones had moved into the estate, that previous November. He had been swimming with him that evening. Thorogood was the one who dove in, somewhat belatedly, to retrieve Jones' body after another house guest, nurse Janet Lawson, saw that he was face down at the bottom of the pool.[6]

There is nothing about this curious incident with the ambulance, or staying with the body until dawn, in Evans' police report of July 3rd. And the wrist injury was not mentioned anywhere in Thorogood's police statement. Evans was not asked to attend the coroner's inquest into Jones' death four days later.

---

[5]   The Final Truth: Who Killed Christopher Robin? by Terry Rawlings (2015) p. 187

[6]   Has the Riddle of Brian Jones' death been solved at last? by Scott Jones, Daily Mail 11/29/08

Anna Wohlin and Frank Thorogood arriving at coroner's inquest

But whoever was directing the activities of the ambulance crew that night decided it was more critical to treat Thorogood's wrist than to transport Jones' body to the morgue. And this circumstance about the wrist injury, and Jones' body laying beside the pool all night, was kept out of the official police reports and coroner's inquest. It is fair to conclude that Thorogood's wrist injury was not likely incurred innocently, when he struggled to lift Jones' body out of the pool. There was never any mention of this by the witnesses who helped lift him out, Janet Lawson and Anna Wohlin (Brian's girlfriend at the estate). Quite probably the injury was from the aftermath of a struggle that had taken place while they were swimming together in the pool- and this is why it had to be kept hidden.

Brian Jones apparently fought for his life as he was being overpowered in that swimming pool. And this caused the injury to Frank Thorogood's wrist. Eventually we will see that there were two other construction workers who, in addition to Thorogood, gang-tackled Jones and held him under water until he was dead.

Thorogood on the morning after the murder

Early on the morning of July 4th, scarcely 24 hours after Brian Jones' body had been carted off of his estate, a bonfire of his possessions was started in the side garden. It burned for many hours and it was huge, according to housekeeper Mary Hallett.

She had lived her whole life at Cotchford and occupied a cottage at its periphery with her teenage daughter and husband Les.

"Michael Martin had got there before me and he told me that they had got the huge bonfire started and were burning all of Brian's things, I don't know why."[7]

Martin, the gardener, also lived in a nearby cottage and, as instructed, was feeding clothing and books and other combustibles into the flames. "A group of men were burning an enormous amount of stuff," he recounted. "I know because I had a very nice little Bible and they'd flung that on, too. Well, I wasn't having that and went immediately and got it out. But, yes, they were burning Brian's things- his clothes, his shirts and what have you. I don't know on whose say so, but they cleared no end of stuff out of his house and burned the lot."[8]

---

[7] Rawlings, p. 112

[8] Golden Stone: The Untold Life and Tragic Death of Brian Jones by Laura Jackson, St. Martin's Press (1992) p. 227

Martin was a deeply-religious man who taught Bible class twice a week in a nearby village. He said that Brian Jones "had this huge leather-bound Bible that he knew back to front... to my knowledge he was reading the Bible every day."[9] He managed to rescue this magnificent Bible when Thorogood brought it out of the house and tossed it into the flames.

Those flames also consumed "substantial amounts of papers and personal items of Brian Jones," according to Stones insider Sam Cutler.[10] Photographs, diaries, legal documents, tapes and demos of impromptu jam sessions and solo compositions- all of this apparently went up in smoke.

What was not consumed by fire was looted. "Everything disappeared from the house," stated Anna Wohlin.[11] Brian had crammed his farmhouse with a near- priceless collection acquired from his many trips to Morocco and the antiques shops of London. There were lavish Persian rugs, hand-carved tables, tapestries, paintings, ornaments- thousands upon thousands of pounds' worth of craftwork that adorned every room.[12]

"Brian had a whole trunk of jewelry," Charlie Watts recalled. "It was like a pirate treasure, a whole trunk full of trinkets."[13] It all disappeared less than 48 hours after his death.

Piles of money vanished from his bedroom. His prolific collection of musical instruments also vanished, excepting his Mellotron and a few guitars that would end up back at the Stones warehouse, and a dulcimer on display at the Rock 'n Roll Hall of Fame. Mick Taylor was stunned to learn he was using one of Brian's favored Firebirds during a recording session for the album *Let It Bleed*. One of his trademark Vox teardrops re-surfaced at the Hard Rock Café in Sacramento in 2007.

The rock star's private museum of antiques, furniture, artwork and other collectibles was witnessed being removed from the house and loaded up by 9:00 AM that morning by Mary Hallett. The builders had parked a low-sided truck next to the house and were busy carting it all off in crates and boxes.

---

9   Rawlings, p. 109
10 From Crimescene to Courtroom by Cyril Wecht, Prometheus Books (2011) p. 162
11 Rawlings, p. 128
12 Ibid p. 99
13 The True Adventures of the Rolling Stones by Stanley Booth, Chicago Review Press (2000) p. 352

Tom Keylock escorting Jones from court in September 1967

Tom Keylock was the man coordinating this heist of Jones' valuables, and the burning of his clothing, papers and mementos. He had been Jones' chauffeur and personal minder since 1966, and had worked himself up to tour manager by 1969. Over 30 years later he claimed he'd been instructed by Jones' own father to remove his son's possessions from the house and burn them.

Keylock walking beside the aftermath of the
burn pile on the afternoon of July 4ᵗʰ

"The only reason I could possibly imagine old man Jones wanting Brian's clothes burned was to stop people getting them and keeping them as some sort of morbid trophy, or for some equally sordid reason."[14]

But when Brian's parents drove out to Cotchford shortly after the coroner's inquest they were shocked to find how little of their son's possessions remained. Mary Hallett had to let them into the locked farmhouse, and they returned home to Cheltenham with only a dozen or so items. It would be particularly egregious of them to have requested that his valuables be burned, since Brian had never married and hadn't made out a will. His parents thereby inherited his sizeable debt, which took well

---

[14] Rawlings, p. 138

7

over a decade to settle. And there is no indication that his five illegitimate children ever received a penny of compensation from his estate, today estimated at $10 million dollars.

Keylock stole for his own purposes the two gold records that Jones kept at the farmhouse. These were for the Stones' first #1 hit, 1963's *Little Red Rooster*- which emphasized Brian's slide guitar- and the 1966 smash *Paint It, Black*- which featured his sitar. These turned up at the Stones Place bar in Toronto in 2003.[15]

A few months after the murder Keylock attempted to influence a well-known music producer in some missing master tapes of Brian's recordings of festival musicians in Morocco. Word of this underhanded deal seeped back to the Stones and he was promptly fired from the organization.[16] These recordings would be released in 1971 as ***Brian Jones Presents the Pipes of Pan at Jojouka.***

---

[15] Trynka, p. 333
[16] Rawlings, p. 155

TWO

JANET LAWSON'S ACCOUNT

Janet Lawson was a registered nurse who arrived at Cotchford late on July 1st to spend a long weekend with her lover, Tom Keylock. He was a married man and already had a son. Janet probably invited herself over to the estate, because her purpose for being there was to inform him that she was pregnant with his child.[17]

The following afternoon, up in the garage apartment, she witnessed Frank Thorogood prepare a drug-laced steak & kidney pie and a large batch of hash cakes. This pie apparently made her sick after she consumed some in the evening meal with Thorogood, Jones and Wohlin.[18]

Shortly after dinner the foursome went outside to relax and have drinks by the pool, and soon enough Brian was encouraging everybody to jump in for a swim. He had been captain of his high school swim team and was a strong and acrobatic swimmer. The pool was comfortably heated to 90 degrees. Lawson declined but Thorogood and Wohlin joined him.

Janet answered a phone call in the kitchen and went back and informed Anna it was for her. She decided to answer it upstairs on the bedroom phone and was pleasantly surprised to be speaking with Terry, one of her fellow Swedish girlfriends living in London.[19]

---

[17] Rawlings, p. 171
[18] Ibid p. 149
[19] The Murder of Brian Jones: The Secret Story of My Love Affair with the Murdered Rolling Stone by Anna Wohlin, Blake Publishing Ltd. (1999) p. 193

As Lawson stated in her police report that evening: "*I returned to the music room in the house and played a guitar. I heard Anna return to the house and talk to the dogs as she went upstairs. I went to the garden and saw the two men were still in the pool. I returned to the house.*

About ten minutes later Frank returned to the house and asked for a towel. I went out to the pool and on the bottom I saw Brian. He was motionless and I sensed the worst straight away."[20]

Janet Lawson the next morning

Lawson went into hiding three weeks later when her housemate, Joan Fitzsimmons, was horrifically injured in a highly-suspicious attack.

---

[20] Statement of Witness, East Grinstead Police Station, July 3, 1969

Fitzsimmons was a taxi driver and frequent visitor to Cotchford and she had intimate knowledge of the circumstances surrounding Brian Jones' death. Lawson would live on an RAF base at her brother's house and gave birth to a daughter in early 1970. She eventually dropped out of nursing and changed her last name to Tallyn.

She was tracked down 35 years later to act as a consultant for the film ***Stoned***, which had been originally titled ***The Wild and Wicked World of Brian Jones***. And she ended up doing three interviews with Jones biographer Terry Rawlings. She admitted to him that she kept in touch with Tom Keylock and even introduced him to her mother over tea. Lawson maintained that Keylock had asked her over to Cotchford 'to keep an eye on Brian'; he was concerned for his health and the tension with Thorogood over unpaid bills.[21]

And she made this same claim to journalist Scott Jones, who did an in-depth sit- down with her in 2008. In all these interviews, Janet Lawson covered up the fact that her pregnancy was what had brought her over to Cotchford. And although she died of cancer 8 months after speaking with Jones, she had no indication of its severity at the time. This breakthrough interview was in no sense a deathbed confession, as Scott Jones himself admitted. Lawson was still covering for Keylock, who was still alive, in poor health himself, and who would decline to talk with Jones for follow-up information.

Lawson confided that her police statement was *"a pack of lies... I was very tired, it was about four or five in the morning."* The officer she had spoken to, Detective Sergeant Peter Hunter, *"suggested most of what I said. It was a load of rubbish."*

"There was something in the air. Frank was acting strangely, throwing his weight around a bit. In the early evening Frank, Anna, Brian and myself had dinner- steak and kidney pie."

After eating, the group returned to the garden where Jones and Thorogood larked about in the pool. Later, when Jones was in the pool by himself, he asked Janet to find his asthma inhaler.

---

[21] Rawlings, pp. 172-174

"*I went to look for it by the pool, in the music room, the reception room and then the kitchen. Frank came in in a lather. His hands were shaking. He was in a terrible state. I thought the worst almost straight away and went to the pool to check.*

When I saw Brian at the bottom of the pool and was calling for help, Frank initially did nothing.

I shouted for Frank again as I ran towards the house, and he burst out before I reached it, ran to the pool and instantly dived in. But I had not said where Brian was. I thought, 'How did he know Brian was at the bottom of the pool?'

I ran back in the house and tried to call 999 but Anna was on the phone and would not get off it."

Did she think Thorogood had killed Jones?

"*Yes. I went into the house to look for Brian's inhaler. Frank jumped back in the pool, <u>did something to Brian</u> and by the time I came back, Brian was lying peacefully on the bottom of the pool with not a ripple in the water.*

I think because of the state Frank was in, something had to have happened. I mean, why would Frank have been standing in the kitchen absolutely terrified if something hadn't happened?"[22]

---

[22] Scott Jones, Daily Mail 11/29/08

Brian Jones shortly before his death

Keylock and Lawson in a heated discussion on the morning of July 3rd

Brian had suffered from asthma since he was a boy and typically left inhalers- squirters he called them- by the corners of his pool. Lawson did draw the conclusion that Thorogood "did something to Brian" while she was out of sight in the house looking for one. Remember, she was careful to make no mention to Scott Jones of her discovered pregnancy. Indeed, she didn't even hint to him that Tom Keylock was on the premises that fateful evening.

Keylock had suffered a stroke in 2008 and early the next year he finally admitted, on camera, after four decades of denial, that "of course I was there, where else would I have been? I had a job to do and I did it."[23] He died a few weeks before Lawson. Curiously enough, it was on the 40th anniversary of Brian Jones' murder, on July 2, 2009. And it appears that Janet Lawson, who hadn't learned yet that she was terminally ill, was giving Scott Jones a bit of a snow job in order to protect the father of her daughter.

On that fateful evening, after leaving the pool area, Janet had apparently gone back to the garage apartment to meet with Tom and further sort out their impending parenthood. Suddenly, they were alerted by disruptive sounds coming from the grounds nearby, highlighted by *girls screaming*.[24] Keylock and Lawson rushed out to the pool area and saw Jones deep and still in the right-hand corner, his blond hair floating up like a halo.

[23] Rawlings, p. 163
[24] Rawlings, p. 171

THREE

JOAN FITZSIMMONS

J oan Fitzsimmons was 29 and grew up in a taxicab family near the coast 50 miles away in Chichester. She shared a house with Janet Lawson, who worked at the hospital there. She began working for Keith Richards and his staff at his nearby Redlands estate in 1967.

Joan was newly divorced but retained her married name and soon began an affair with a builder at Redlands named Frank Thorogood, who had a wife back in North London. Thorogood had a rental in town and his landlady, Joanna Laidlow, eventually walked and cared for the dogs of both Richards and Jones at their respective estates. And she became a good friend and pub companion of Joan Fitzsimmons.

It was in one of the Chichester pubs that Janet Lawson was introduced to Tom Keylock, and they became regular double-daters with Fitzsimmons and Thorogood. And after Thorogood was fired by Richards for suspected thievery, he was foisted via Keylock onto the unsuspecting Jones.[25]

"Joan was very fond of Frank and she spent a lot of time with him," Laidlow stated. "She was driving him to East Grinstead and London. Joan would also take me to and fro, doing dog business. The affair was quite happy for a year and a half, up until Christmas 1968-69."

"Joan was lovely," Mary Hallett recalled. "She was a very popular young lady in her early twenties and much in awe of Brian."

---

[25] Rawlings, p. 170

"Brian and Joan grew very fond of each other," said her brother John Russell.[26]

That Christmas she picked up a fare at the Chichester railway station and took him to where he had seen an advertisement for work, at a nearby school. He was 19, a native of Jordan with dark and curly hair who had never been in the area before.

They fell in love immediately and she invited him to stay with her. His name was Michael Ziyadeh.

Redlands estate

"Early in 1969 they even took off on a holiday together in Tangier," Janet Lawson related. "Joan was doing work for Brian and she frequently took her Jordanian friend with her to Cotchford. This chap and Brian liked each other a lot- Brian gave him money and some of his clothes. Joan was running all kinds of errands for Brian, driving up and down, and she often left her boyfriend at Cotchford for the whole day. He would wander around the garden for hours asking the builders for a drink every now and then. That's how Brian and this chap became friends."[27]

---

[26] Ibid pp. 176-177
[27] Rawlings, p. 178

Joan Fitzsimmons   *Michael Ziyadeh*

Frank Thorogood was humiliated by this romantic misadventure. He was bald and over the hill and knew he couldn't compete. His jealousy flared to an angry tirade one day by the poolside, a few weeks before Jones' death. Joan was raising his ire by flirting with Michael and as Frank ranted Brian suddenly "pushed Frank fully clothed into the swimming pool." This incident may have led to the black eye Fitzsimmons soon received from her young boyfriend.

Ziyadeh spent July 2nd on the grounds at Cotchford and Fitzsimmons, who had spent the day running errands, picked him up at 9:00 PM sharp. They drove back to Chichester and retired for the night. But she was awoken at 6:00 AM by a call from Thorogood. In an emotional, half-drunken outburst he confessed to killing Brian Jones. He told her everything that had happened and said the grounds were full of police and asked her to come over for emotional support.

A few days later Fitzsimmons and Ziyadeh met up in a Chichester pub with Janet Lawson and Joanna Laidlow to discuss what details they knew about that dreadful night at Cotchford. There was talk about whether or not they should go to the press and word of this leaked back to Thorogood and Keylock.

"Joan told me she was not frightened of the Jordanian boy but it was everyone else who was causing the trouble between them," a relative confided to police investigators, *before her attack*. "She then said that she was frightened of Frank and she started talking about the death of Brian Jones. She said things were not as they appear… if it got out that she thought this then she would be the next one. She said she could make some money out of it, because she could go to the papers about it."[28]

Joan's mother added, "Frank said to me, 'Joan knows a lot of stuff that shouldn't get out. I've heard from somewhere that she and Joanna Laidlow were supposed to be going to the newspapers'." And her mom tacked on this confidential tidbit: "I know Joan left the house about half an hour before Brian Jones was drowned."

On July 9th, the day before Jones' funeral, Thorogood went down to Chichester and located the distraught Fitzsimmons. He chased her through traffic and the town's back streets until she got to Joanna Laidlow's house, where she barricaded herself inside. There she contacted a relative who managed to pull him away and then drove him all the way back to London.

On July 26th Joan was discovered on a beach a few miles south of Chichester. She was in a coma with a fractured skull and wounds that left her permanently blinded. She had been bludgeoned to within an inch of her life with a large stone found nearby.

Before   *After*

---

[28] Rawlings, p. 181

Her boyfriend Michael was arrested the next day, hiding down the beach in blood- stained clothes. He pled guilty to attempted murder and did four years in Broadmoor prison before being deported. Yet he always claimed he did not carry out the attack. The police concluded that "the motive for this remains a mystery."[29]

Indeed, it may have been a set-up. As Janet Lawson observed, "Frank and Tom knew all the thugs in North London. If there was a dirty job to do, they knew the right person to carry it out."[30] Thorogood was interviewed twice by police but claimed that, on the day in question, he'd been in a North London pub, "in the company of my friend and Stones manager Tom Keylock." His alibi was corroborated by his wife.

There is a hefty amount of paperwork pertaining to this case that has disappeared from the official record. Public access has been denied at the National Archives by the Crown Protection Service, which cites the harm that may be done to living persons from having embarrassing details about their sex lives revealed. Making use of "the 75-year rule" they will be kept private until 2044- at the least.

Fitzsimmons eventually recovered sufficiently to speak with police three times about what she knew about Thorogood's possible role in her attack and in the death of Brian Jones. This information has never been made available. Records for what she related in 1992 for a BBC *Crimewatch* documentary about the Jones mystery have apparently been destroyed. Also missing is her brother's attestation in regards to her fear of Thorogood.

Ziyadeh, when visited in prison by police investigators, denied having any knowledge pertaining to the death of Brian Jones. Ziyadeh's statements have disappeared from the official files. His cellmate, however, Edward Patrick Coyle, spoke separately with an investigator on August 10, 1969- he claimed that during some late-night revelations Ziyadeh had told him further secrets about the attack on his girlfriend. And that he knew who had murdered Brian Jones. These details were never made public- although Coyle's story was carried in a local newspaper- and subsequent police investigation determined it was based upon "unfounded gossip and hearsay."

---

[29] Scott Jones, Daily Mail 11/29/08
[30] Rawlings, p. 180

Joan Fitzsimmons died in 2002. Her 9:00 PM departure from Cotchford on the evening of July 2nd appears to receive some tentative support from the recollections of Les and Mary Hallett, who occupied a cottage at the edge of the estate.

"There was a terrific lot of screaming coming from down there," Mary remembered, "awful screaming and then car doors slamming and then cars screeching away. I sent Les out to see what was going on, and these cars were off down the lane and then there was silence."[31]

Les Hallett said it was quite dark by then and "around ten" when the ruckus woke him and his wife. "We are only a couple of hundred yards up on the right and so we were used to hearing a lot of noise from down there, this night was very noisy so I went out into the lane and all these cars were screeching by in reverse out the drive and tearing off down the lane."[32]

The problem though, like so much in this case, is that these recollections may instead be complete fiction. A more accurate scenario at the Hallett cottage was apparently discerned by Trevor Hobley, the president of the Brian Jones Fan Club- which disbanded in 2010. He recorded interviews with both Les and Mary Hallett and each of them denied ever hearing screaming, or cars screeching away, at 10:00 PM. "In actual fact it was after midnight that they were awakened by their teenage daughter who saw the flashing blue police lights reflected in the sky."[33]

So we can, perhaps, tentatively dismiss the squealing cars and girls as embellishments that distract from the barebones truth. And keep our focus on the timeframe a couple of hours before midnight.

[31] Rawlings, p. 110
[32] Ibid p. 146
[33] Brian Jones Fan Club statement from Trevor Hobley, 11/17/05

FOUR

THE BUILDERS

Frank Thorogood was an old school friend of Tom Keylock's and in 1967 he was hired to work at Redlands. Keith Richards wanted his newly-purchased estate, with its thatched roof surrounded by a moat, upgraded to the quality befitting a major rock star. But Frank and his team took advantage of their plush working conditions and began rummaging through drawers and pilfering things, "not doing very much work at all."[34] Richards was never happy with their work anyway and eventually fired them all. Keylock dumped them off on Brian Jones, who was looking for repairs and an upgrade at his own Cotchford Farm.

But the malicious behavior continued. Early in January Brian and his girlfriend Suki Potier took a holiday in Ceylon, at the home of science-fiction writer Arthur C. Clarke. They returned to find the Cotchford house a royal mess, with empty liquor bottles and dirty dishes scattered all over the place. Piles of cash soon began vanishing from the bedroom. Expensive furnishings disappeared. And Thorogood also resorted to psychological harassment, flashing a strobe light into the bedroom late at night. A dead cat was left in the kitchen cupboard with its eyes poked out. Suki had had enough by April and moved out.

Thorogood used the occasion to emigrate from his garage apartment, which he shared with three of his builders, and take up a room in the house proper. "They were just pulling the place apart and not putting it back together again," Michael Martin recalled. "They would start drinking at

---

[34] Rawlings, p. 165

about midday every day, starting off with a few beers, then wine, then it would be anything goes… and that would be that for another day." Hard liquor and cases of beer would be charged to the village store and then delivered to Cotchford, courtesy of Brian's Stones account.

"[Thorogood] did absolutely nothing all day," a friend who visited the farmhouse related. "There were no signs of construction work going on at all. He was just wandering around like part of the scenery."[35]

Yet Brian was a hapless drunk who couldn't bring himself to get rid of this dodgy gang of builders. Jones was a late riser who kept to himself most of the time. "He loved his garden and he would walk around in a huge sheepskin coat with a bottle of vodka in his breast pocket," said one of his carper-fitters, David Gibson.

He "seemed to have something on his mind and seemed to be hiding away" at Cotchford. Brian complained that he was "a prisoner in his own home" and even expressed fears that he would be killed. "I got the impression he was scared of Frank who was bossy and domineering… It was as if Frank was in control of everything at the house."[36]

Brian would get locked out of his own house, and it wasn't from misplacing his own keys. "We would go out shopping," Mrs. Hallett recalled, "and when we came back he would be sitting there waiting for us. He would be lost because there was no one in the house to let him in."[37]

In June, during a bitter dispute over money, Thorogood threw Jones out of his own kitchen.[38] Anna Wohlin witnessed, more than once, the conniving builder rummaging through Jones' private demos with musicians like Jimi Hendrix and John Lennon.[39] At the end of that month a kitchen beam came crashing down and narrowly missed her head.[40]

---

[35] Ibid pp. 107-109

[36] 'Why I Still Believe Brian Jones Was Murdered', The Argus, 7/4/00; Is this proof Brian Jones was murdered? Fifty years after the Rolling Stone was found dead in his swimming pool, a new TV documentary re-examines evidence in the case by Alison Boshoff, Daily Mail 7/3/19

[37] Rawlings, p. 103

[38] Ibid p. 166

[39] Wecht, p. 154

[40] Wohlin, pp. 171-172

Unfortunately Wohlin was too heavily under the influence of drugs and alcohol on the night of Jones' murder to remember much in the way of specific details. Her 1999 memoir reads like a paperback dime-store romance with few original facts in it. She was persuaded in her July 3rd police statement to believe she had dove into the pool to retrieve Jones' body, and she even claimed to have felt his hand grasp hers as she applied artificial respiration.

Yet on the basis of Janet Lawson's 2008 account, Wohlin was still upstairs on the phone and oblivious to what transpired in the pool. Thorogood was the one who dove in to get the body and Lawson & Wohlin helped lift it out of the pool. Perhaps the key memory of Anna's was the phone call she received from London that had drawn her away and left Jones alone with the one-eyed Thorogood. She was whisked off to Stockholm by Rolling Stones management on the day of Brian's funeral and didn't attend. Wohlin signed what essentially was a non-disclosure agreement and may have been given a substantial amount of hush money.[41]

A friend of hers, Jim Carter-Fae, had this contrasting recollection, which casts quite some doubt on Janet Lawson's seemingly solid account. Carter-Fae was the manager of the Speakeasy, a popular rock 'n roll club where Anna had been a dancer. She called him the night it happened and "she was very upset." She told him "**she had gone upstairs <u>to sleep</u>, then suddenly she came down. *Frank and the nurse were standing by the pool, Brian was there and they were doing nothing at all*.** Anna dove in and tried to fish him out. Brian was floating in the water under the pool and they wouldn't help her at all. They were just standing by the pool watching."

"She was moved out of the country so fast that it wasn't true, and told to say nothing."[42]

---

[41] Wohlin, pp. 213-229
[42] Rawlings, p. 128

Garage apartment at left

Frank and his nephew Danny had originally started at Redlands, and they lodged at the home of Joanna Laidlow. Upon the recommendation of Joan Fitzsimmons, he hired a couple of Chichester locals, John Betsworth and Morris Tucker.[43] "They weren't real builders," Mary Hallett said. "More like jacks of all trades."[44]

Johnny Betsworth was a short but powerfully built man who had the same birthday, February 28th, as Brian Jones. He got blind drunk and threw up all over himself when Jones took them all out to the local pub to celebrate.[45] Mo Tucker was Fitzsimmons' next-door neighbor and, unbeknownst to her, a police informant. His information helped instigate a police raid on Redlands that led to a well-publicized trial of Keith Richards and Mick Jagger for marijuana possession.

---

[43] Rawlings, p. 165
[44] Ibid p. 106
[45] Ibid p. 166

Thorogood and his gang moved into Cotchford virtually in unison and used the garage apartment as a haven for their extramarital love trysts. "Mo and Johnny practically moved straight in with Frank and they were the most unfaithful chaps that ever walked. They were all married," Hallett recounted. "I've seen Mo sitting with a girl on his knee, cuddling her and talking to his wife on the phone saying, 'I'll see you on such and such a day, I'm very busy at the moment'."[46]

"I would watch them just help themselves to everything, go in Brian's cupboards and take things off the shelves, put them in their bags and off they would go. So many things would disappear."[47] Keylock had arranged for Thorogood to charge purchases to Jones' London account and besides booze, the builders would also buy furniture for their personal use.

And then there were the threats. "Mo threatened to fill me in if I made a fuss about what I saw them doing," the gardener related. "They had threatened to rearrange my face a couple of times for what they considered my sticking my nose in."

Four or five times that June an old friend from the Cheltenham rhythm & blues circuit, Alexis Korner, stopped by to visit Brian. He had managed a club and a band and was a mentor for Brian's rising stardom. Brian "talked at length about the bad feeling between himself and the builders. He was keen to point out the parts of the house that, supposedly, had been either refurbished or renovated. He would point to this part or that saying, 'That cost me such and such'." Korner noted that these particular parts of the house were either half-finished or left untouched.[48]

Brian was apparently screwing himself up to get rid of them for keeps and it seems they knew this was coming. The day before his death, Mary Hallett overheard a threatening conversation between Anna and the builders as she went about her housework: "They were discussing Brian and saying how he'd be so and so and they'd do so and so and he'd be sorry… I couldn't help but hear something about what they'd do to him."[49]

---

[46] Ibid p. 100
[47] Ibid p. 106
[48] Ibid p. 103
[49] Rawlings, p. 124

Mo Tucker and Tom Keylock, with Frank Thorogood in the doorway

The next day, July 2nd, Brian was resolved to finally fire the whole gang. He invited a few friends over for enhanced personal security. Although once a notorious drug abuser, Brian had sworn them off and visitors to his estate could be expected to be searched for illegal narcotics.[50]

Suki Potier drove up about 5:00 PM and three of her girlfriends soon followed.[51] The drummer for the Walker Brothers, Gary Leeds, was already there. As was Michael Ziyadeh, who had been left all day by Joan Fitzsimmons. Another taxi driver for Jones, Jackie Shaw, was also on the premises.

Inside the music room at the farmhouse David Gibson was laying carpet with his partner Eddie Loakes. A third carpet-fitter, Horace Fox, was alleged to also be there in the 1994 book ***Paint It, Black*** but was likely an invention of that book. Gibson owned his business and worked independently of the builders. He told police that he didn't know Fox and he wasn't aware of anyone else in the house then.[52]

---

[50] Wecht, pp. 152-153
[51] Rawlings, pp. 110, 125
[52] Ibid p. 239

Wohlin contends that Jones had actually fired Thorogood on June 30th, the morning after the beam came crashing down in the kitchen. He contacted the Stones office and asked for copies of his bills and that payments to Thorogood be stopped. While the crew repaired the damage Brian began to feel guilty about the consequences for their families.[53]

Rawlings makes no mention of the beam incident; instead he put forth that Thorogood had visited the Stones office in London that July 2nd. He returned to the small gathering at Cotchford finally realizing that his employment had indeed been finally terminated. He took his crew down to the town pub to brood over these developments, and purchased further bottles of booze before returning to Jones' estate.[54]

Thorogood believed he was owed almost £8,000, and he needed to pay his workmates. They had been making well over 10 times the going rate for tradesmen in the late 60s. Jones had already dished out £18,000 to them since November, a monstrous sum which approaches £300,000 at today's values.[55]

Anger over unpaid money, Rawlings argues, is what brought Thorogood to drown Jones in the pool later that evening. This hypothesis neglects, however, the sad fact that he would likely get no money at all if Jones was dead. The tensions at Cotchford had been ongoing for months and the real motive went deeper than disbursements that would eventually get settled.

In any event, the party-goers were asked to leave the premises fairly early. This seems to have been at the behest of Jones' minder, Tom Keylock, who had been on the estate since at least the night of July 1st, to greet Janet Lawson.

As David Gibson related decades later, "[Brian] said there was a person there quite constantly called Tom, who he said called himself a road manager, who was extremely friendly with the builders. We wanted to work late that night but *we were asked to leave*, as they were having a rave up that evening."[56]

A Keith Richards interview two years after the fact lends some corroboration to Gibson's account. "There were a lot of chicks there and

---

[53] Wohlin, pp. 177-181
[54] Rawlings, pp. 136, 146
[55] Boshoff, Daily Mail 7/4/19
[56] Rawlings, p. 168

there was a whole thing going on, they were having a party… [I] wanted to know who was there and couldn't find out. The only cat I could ask was *the one I think who got rid of everybody* and did the whole disappearing trick so that when the cops arrived, it was just an accident."[57]

Keith Richards in 1971

So the grounds were essentially cleared once Fitzsimmons picked up Ziyadeh at 9:00 PM. And then the main house guests could sit down to a steak & kidney pie, spiked with an unknown drug by Thorogood. This may have been what led Wohlin to start falling asleep after she was called away from the poolside, as she described later that evening to Carter-Fae. And Lawson's time away is similarly indeterminate, if she was connecting with Keylock in the garage apartment.

Gibson told police in 1994 that he had last seen Jones at 9:00 PM and he "appeared to be sober and in good condition."[58] This was extended to 10:00 PM for his 2000 *Argus* interview: "…and I remember he called out to me from the landing window, 'See you in the morning, Dave'." Gibson added that he received a phone call at 7:00 AM the next morning saying he was no longer needed and would be paid in full. A few days later he

---

[57] Keith Richards, The Rolling Stone Interview, Rolling Stone 8/19/71
[58] Rawlings, p. 239

received an envelope with his payment and an extra £200 with a note saying 'Take a holiday'.[59]

Trevor Hobley discovered that Jones had actually called the carpet-fitters back into the house, and they had a conversation in the music room for an additional 25 minutes. Brian was terrified for his life and pleaded with them to spend the night.

Two nights before Jones had apparently holed up in a hotel in London. He was in the company of a blond girl, making plans to leave the country.[60] There he ran into the musician Graham Bond, a fellow alumnus of Alexis Korner's band *Blues Incorporated*. Once Bond and his girlfriend were brought to his hotel room Brian sobbed, "They're going to kill me!!" When asked who was going to kill him, Jones named him names that Rawlings wouldn't reproduce "for legal reasons".[61] There is no mention of this incident in Anna Wohlin's book.

During these last desperate days Brian also sent a telegram to Stones publicist Les Perrin, letting him know in no uncertain terms that he was in fear for his life.[62]

---

[59] The Argus, 7/4/00
[60] Hobley, 11/17/05
[61] Rawlings, p. 173
[62] Ibid p. 123

Word slowly spilled out over the years that Thorogood's builders had been present at the time of Jones' death. And may have been directly involved.

In a 1991 letter to a researcher, Detective Chief Inspector Robert Marshall wrote that "[Jones] was at the farmhouse with six or so associates"- thus revealing that there were more than three witnesses at the scene of his death.[63]

The following year Joan Fitzsimmons alerted the producer of the *Crimewatch* documentary that not only was Mo Tucker a police informant, also there but that he had given an interview to police shortly after Jones' drowning. This information disappeared.

Tucker, in fact, had contacted his liaison officer the night of the death.[64] Decades later, Stones insider Sam Cutler received a copy of this officer's notebook. It listed the names of all the people at the Cotchford estate when he arrived on the murder scene.[65]

One of the officers who drove up there soon after first responder Albert Evans- just ahead of DCI Marshall- was a drugs squad officer named Richard Burchman. He recalled that "When we arrived at Cotchford a group of men introduced themselves as builders."[66] Yet not a single statement was ever taken from them.

Frank Thorogood died in 1993 and made a presumptuous deathbed confession to Tom Keylock that "It was me who done Brian." But this wasn't mentioned until the *Crimewatch* documentary three months later. Thorogood's daughter, Jan Bell, not only doubted that he had spent any time alone with her father. Her father had been admitted to the hospital for a respiratory problem and wasn't even aware that he was on his deathbed.[67]

Johnny Betsworth died in 1983. Mo Tucker died in 2001, the day after a real estate sale that made him a very wealthy man.[68] And no one alive could contest Keylock when, advising for the 2000 film *Stoned*, he stated

[63] Scott Jones, Daily Mail 11/29/08
[64] Rawlings, p. 189
[65] Ibid p. 169
[66] Ibid p. 186
[67] Trynka, p. 329
[68] Rawlings, p. 165

that "Frank committed this crime with Mo and Johnny looking on!"[69] This was bolstered by an e-mail Rawlings received from Tucker's widow: "By the way did Tommie tell you Mo was there when they did Brian in? He was surly, was my own Mister Tucker!"[70]

It can be concluded with confidence that at the time of Brian Jones' murder there were at least six people at his estate- Wohlin, Lawson, Thorogood, Keylock, Tucker and Betsworth. Yet only the initial three made it into the official police accounts of his death. And after the night's interrogations, they were prepared to charge Frank Thorogood with murder. Which is probably what led him to telephone Joan Fitzsimmons and confess to her what he'd done.

"The police sergeant that was in charge said that he intended to make an arrest," Mary Hallett recalled.[71] But instead they let him go.

The builders continued to use Cotchford Farm as their main meeting place through the end of July.[72] On the day of the funeral they had stood together at the back of St. Mary's during the church service.[73] Later they all cozied up to the immediate family as the coffin was being lowered into the ground.

---

[69] Ibid p. 189

[70] Ibid p. 167

[71] Ibid p. 137

[72] Rawlings, pp. 189-190

[73] Ibid p. 179

Tom Keylock behind parents Louisa & Lewis Jones, Frank Thorogood and his nephew Danny behind Brian's grandmother, Barbara Jones, Suki Potier, Morris Tucker and Johnny Betsworth at the far right behind an unidentified aunt.

FIVE

NICHOLAS FITZGERALD

Nicholas Fitzgerald's story begins with the story of his cousin, doomed Guinness heir Tara Browne.

Browne was the second son of the aristocrat Dominick Browne, the 4th baron of Oranmore and Browne, and Oonagh Guinness, an heir to the Guinness brewery fortune. Dominick had sat in the English House of Lords since 1927. Oonagh owned a tract of about eight square miles beside Lough Tay in the Wicklow Mountains, south of Dublin, known as the Luggala Estate.

Tara co-owned a London clothing shop called Dandy Fashions and ingratiated himself into the swinging social scene of the trend-setting 60s, making friends with the Beatles, the Rolling Stones, Jimi Hendrix, David Bowie, Peter Sellers, Michael Caine, Salvador Dali and J. Paul Getty, Jr. He was a prolific drug user and is credited with introducing Paul McCartney to LSD; one of McCartney's pianos had the same psychedelic pattern painted as one of Browne's cars.

Brian Jones was so close to Tara that they would joke they were brothers. They spent so much time together people wondered whether they were having an affair. Brian and his girlfriend at the time, Anita Pallenberg, did take several LSD trips with Tara,[74] whose girlfriend was a Pallenberg lookalike, a 19-year-old model named Suki Potier.

For his 21st birthday in 1966 Tara invited Brian and Anita and a host of other luminaries to celebrate at the castlelike hunting lodge on his

---

[74] Trynka, p. 193

family estate. The drugs were plentiful along with the best liquor, as the Lovin' Spoonful serenaded aristocrats and the long-haired scruffs of the 60s counterculture. He was poised to begin tapping into a £ million trust fund in four more years.[75]

Tara Browne   *with Anita Pallenberg*

But a week before Christmas his glamorous dreams came to a sudden end. He ran a red light and crashed his turquoise Lotus Elan into a parked van. Suki, who was unscathed, wrapped her coat around Tara as he lay dying. The accident was memorialized the next year in the Beatles' opus *A Day in the Life.*

… he hadn't noticed that the lights had changed…

[75] 'A BOY WHO HAD EVERYTHING' The tragic rich kid whose car crash inspired The Beatles' classic A Day in the Life by Antonella Lazzeri, The Sun 10/23/16

Nicholas Fitzgerald had attended that gala birthday party at the Guinness family estate in 1966. He was three years younger than his

cousin and had met Brian Jones the previous summer. He soon became a habitual friend who shared numerous phone calls, barstools, backstage encounters, hotel parties and occasional drug and sexual escapades.

Early in the evening of July 1st, 1969, Suki Potier contacted Fitzgerald at his apartment in London. She explained that Brian had telephoned her three times lately, fearful that he was in some kind of danger. She asked Nicholas if he could go out to Cotchford and check and see if he was alright.[76] Fitzgerald enlisted his personal assistant, a 19-year-old student named Richard Cadbury, to drive him out to Hartfield the next day.

They arrived about 1:30 PM and decided to have lunch in the town pub, the Hay Waggon. Sure enough, Brian Jones had the same idea and he walked in with a construction worker shortly after they arrived. They were surprised to see each other.

In the pub's urinal Jones managed to confide that he was "being followed, watched… It's as if I work for *them*. But there's someone behind them, telling them to watch me. There's got to be," he emphasized. "Can you help me?"

"Some days they hide my motorcycle. When I'm on the phone, the line will suddenly go dead… They're always leaping up to answer the phone and then they tell me it was a wrong number."

"Please stay with me tonight, Nicholas. Just to hold me."[77]

When they got back to the bar, the construction worker had disappeared and left his unfinished beer on the counter. Fitzgerald offered to give the

---

[76] Brian Jones: The Inside Story of the Original Rolling Stone by Nicholas Fitzgerald, G.P. Putnam's Sons, New York (1985) pp. 7-8

[77] Ibid, pp. 13-14

paranoid Jones a lift right back to Cotchford, only a mile away. When they got there they noticed two of the workers installing floodlights around the pool.

They spent the afternoon relaxing outside on some garden furniture and Brian told him about his plans for his new band, which would delve into a mixture of jazz, rhythm & blues, gospel and Moroccan music. Then they went into his music studio where he played demos of jam sessions with Lennon and Hendrix. And Jones added that, "Things keep disappearing around here. Last week I spent over twenty hours working on a single tape and now I can't find it."[78]

After being interrupted by a phone call Jones returned holding a scrap of paper and asked Fitzgerald to pick up a girl at the Hayward Heaths train station a dozen miles away. He read the name, "Luciana Martinez Delarosa". She would be in the lounge at the Hayward Hotel.

Fitzgerald and Cadbury arrived at the hotel about 7:40 PM but saw no sign of Delarosa. And they asked around but found no indication that she'd ever even been at the station. They opted to keep on waiting and had a couple of drinks and eventually phoned Cotchford to see if she'd shown up there.

---

[78] Fitzgerald, p. 20

It was getting close to 10:00 PM. A woman answered "Hello?" and Nicholas asked to speak with Brian. He didn't recognize her voice, but noticed no kind of foreign accent. He could hear music and talking and laughter in the background as he held the line for about three minutes until it suddenly hung up.

They decided to return to the Cotchford estate and arrived back there shortly after 11:00 PM. But they were blocked from entering there, blinded by a set of headlights near the top of the driveway. It was a foreign car, left-hand drive, vacated, and its driver's side door was wide open. The lights from the farmhouse were on but the place was silent.

Cadbury whispered, "There's something going on. Let's go through the trees." So they avoided the driveway and groped through the brambles and thicket that surrounded the property, making their way for the pool area at the rear of the farmhouse.

"We got glimpses of light through the leaves. We emerged behind the beamed stone wall of the summer house in shadows, where we heard muffled voices. We skirted the summer house, came around to its side and saw the full glare of the lights now over the pool and in the windows of the house. We had a clear view of the pool and of what was going on there. And what the hell **was** going on?

At the far right-hand corner of the swimming pool three men were standing. They were dressed in sweaters and jeans. Their clothes gave the impression they were workmen. The power of the spotlights blotted out their features and made their faces look like white blobs. The moment I became aware of them, the middle one dropped to his knees, reached into the water and pushed down on the top of a head that looked white.

At the opposite corner of the pool- far left- stood two other people, a man and a woman, gazing down into the pool where the kneeling man was pushing down on the head, keeping it under. The man to the right of the kneeling man said something. It sounded like a command and I caught the words "… do something." At that, the third man on that side jumped into the water the way an animal might jump, arms outstretched, knees bent. He landed on the back of the struggling swimmer. The man who snapped out the command seemed to be preparing himself also to jump in.

Breathless, unbelieving, paralyzed, I looked at the man and woman. She was standing a little in his shadow and I couldn't see her face. But why didn't they move? Do something? They looked like extras on a film set, waiting to play their parts.

Out of the bushes right next to us stepped a burly man wearing glasses. He pushed Richard out of the way. He grabbed my shoulder. His other hand made a fist, which he put in my face menacingly.

"Get the hell out of here, Fitzgerald, or you'll be next," he growled. It was a Cockney accent. I was terrified. He meant it. There was no way I could do battle with him. He turned me around and pushed me hard back into the woods. I almost fell, but went stumbling blindly into the darkness under the trees. Ahead of me I heard the rustle and the swish as Cadbury went struggling away."[79]

The man with the Cockney accent was Jones' minder Tom Keylock, and Fitzgerald recognized the same voice three days later at a concert the

---

[79] Fitzgerald, pp. 240-241

Stones gave in the Hyde Park section of London. In a tribute to Brian, Keylock was attempting to release thousands of butterflies, but half of them fell dead right out of their cartons. "That was a bloody stupid idea, wasn't it?" he muttered and Fitzgerald overheard him from the edge of the stage.[80]

Keylock openly admitted to Terry Rawlings that he had found two men in the bushes that night and thrown them off the property. But he maintained this had happened in the wee hours of the morning. His language had been a bit more colorful; he had actually said, "Fuck off, Fitzgerald, or you'll be next!"[81]

But Keylock had, in fact, already been named in an August 1983 statement that Fitzgerald gave to Sussex police detective J.F. Reece:

"FITZGERALD claimed that he saw THOROGOOD by the side of the pool fully dressed and two other men not known to him pushing JONES into the pool. FITZGERALD goes on to describe the scene including the fact that a blonde haired girl was present and that she was screaming. FITZGERALD then claimed that he and CADBURY were surprised by a man believed to

---

[80]   Ibid p. 250
[81]   Rawlings, pp. 138, 148, 173

be connected with the publicity of the group and a man that he refers to as possibly Tom KEYLOCK. KEYLOCK is apparently said to have threatened FITZGERALD and CADBURY that they would be next if they didn't leave. FITZGERALD claims that he and CADBURY immediately drove back to London.

Detective Chief Superintendent REECE was of the view that FITZGERALD was a 'Walter Mitty' type character and discussion with those officers who attended the scene indicated that when they arrived no other person was present other than JONES' girlfriend, THOROGOOD and LAWSON.

It would seem that FITZGERALD is intending to write a book about the death of Brian JONES and that the surrounding publicity would help the sales of the book."

Fitzgerald refused to sign his police statements. He gave three, but only a portion of one has survived. Reece informed him several times that he might become an accessory after the fact by withholding information. Yet Fitzgerald contended that he himself had escaped murder attempts and that his friend, Richard Cadbury, had died "in mysterious circumstances".[82]

The Sussex police of 1983 had closed their initial 1969 investigation (and coverup) and couldn't be persuaded, without hard evidence to the contrary, that re-opening the Brian Jones case was warranted. *"All we have here are unsubstantiated allegations from a man who will not make a statement, and whose memory, temperament and motives are questionable."* And so they dismissed Fitzgerald as a fantasist who was seeking to drum up publicity for his 1985 book. It had little success and was likewise dismissed as of questionable veracity.

A review here of what Fitzgerald claimed to have witnessed that night might be in order. The three men in work clothes at the right side of the swimming pool is a clear allusion to Frank Thorogood, Mo Tucker and Johnny Betsworth- whose presence there has already been independently established. The man and woman at the other side of the pool were in all likelihood Tom Keylock and Janet Lawson.

---

[82] Trynka, p. 326

This ties in with what Anna Wohlin had told Jim Carter-Fae that same night (although his recollection mixed up Thorogood and Keylock): "Frank and the nurse were standing by the pool. Brian was there and they were doing nothing." It was apparently Lawson's screams, mentioned in Fitzgerald's police account, that roused Wohlin out of her drowsiness to race downstairs to the pool.

Two phone calls that night are suspicious and may have involved an unknown accomplice in London. At about 7:00 PM "Luciana Martinez Delarosa" called Brian Jones, which served as an excuse to get Fitzgerald and Cadbury off the Cotchford estate. And shortly before 11:00 PM, a Swedish friend from London phoned Anna Wohlin, which served to get her away from the pool area. Lawson soon followed and met with Keylock in the garage apartment. What she related to journalist Scott Jones in 2008 was essentially a load of rubbish, crafted so as to protect the father of her love child, Tom Keylock.

Richard Cadbury was scared off by the whole episode and quickly disappeared from Nicholas Fitzgerald's life. Shortly thereafter an unnamed underworld character advised him against going to the police, since Jones' death had "been in the cards a long time, anyway."[83] Fitzgerald kept his silence until selling his story to the tabloid *News of the World* in February 1983, which was reiterated in the *Gloucestershire Echo* that June. He drifted into obscurity and died of alcoholism in 2009.

Even though his story was widely dismissed as clever but untrue, Nicholas Fitzgerald knew many details of what happened at Cotchford that night that didn't come to light until many years later.

Trevor Hobley had this important addendum. He noted that the swimming pool episode in Fitzgerald's book, 16 years after the event, was actually written by one of his ghostwriters, Bernard Toms. Fitzgerald had made a verbal statement, sometime prior to getting his book published, that he and Cadbury had actually seen three men holding a body upside down with the head in a trough of water.[84]

---

[83] Fitzgerald, pp. 246-247
[84] Brian Jones Fan Club statement from Trevor Hobley, 11/17/05

SIX

KEYLOCK

Tom Keylock, born in 1926, was the youngest paratrooper at the battle of Arnhem in the Netherlands in 1944. He began with the Stones through a car-hire company he owned in North London, acting as their chauffeur, minder and self-described "hardman". The burly fixer with the Cockney accent was characterized as "half protecting angel, half Mafioso" and commonly regarded as "a shifty bastard".[85]

Employed by the Rolling Stones office, he became Keith Richards' driver and bodyguard at Redlands. But in due course he was fired. "Keith had bought some furniture, and Keylock put his own furniture on the bill," Sam Cutler recalled. "He was a low-life."[86]

---

[85] Trynka, p. 219
[86] Ibid p. 311

But Keylock had his own code of honor and was not afraid to use combat techniques he'd acquired in the British Army. He once knocked another driver's teeth out after an argument over a stolen camera. The favor was returned, indirectly, during a concert in Athens four days before a military coup. Police stormed the stadium stage after only five songs and stopped the show. Bouquets of red carnations Keylock had tossed into the audience were taken as fomenting communism, and he lost five teeth in the ensuing chaos.[87]

He was transferred over to Brian Jones in time to accompany him, Anita Pallenberg and Christopher Gibbs, an antiques dealer, on a trip to Tangier in August 1966.

Gibbs recalled, "I don't think Tom liked Brian very much. He didn't seem to like music very much. He was meant to be working for Brian but he was really there for his own good always. He wasn't interested in looking after Brian, just interested in what he could make out of the situation. He was the type that would sell stories to the newspapers."[88]

Six months later, on another trip to Morocco, Keylock played an integral part in a ruse that enabled Keith Richards and Anita Pallenberg to whisk off to London as newfound lovebirds. Leaving Brian abandoned

---

[87] "The Botched Rolling Stones Show in Athens 4 Days Before the April 21, 1967 Coup," by Philip Chrysopolous, Greek Reporter, 4/21/18

[88] Rawlings, p. 118

in a foreign country, devoid not only of his girlfriend of two years. He was also devoid of his wallet, and had no identification or money at hand.

This caper solidified Keylock's gravitas within the Stones organization and he recruited and hired his own close-knit network of hardmen who would answer to him. "The Stones have always loved gangsters and had these shitheads working with them," Cutler observed.

A drug raid in May of 1968 found a wad of cannabis resin in a ball of wool in Brian's London apartment. While awaiting trial he spent a month sequestered away at the Redlands estate, while Keith and Anita were holidaying abroad. Jones was under the strict supervision of Keylock, who despised him.[89]

Their warden/inmate resentful dynamic spilled over into Cotchford, where Keylock moved in just after Jones. Even the gardener noticed he didn't like him and Keylock was opposed when Anna Wohlin moved in that June.

"I don't employ the bloody man, Nicholas," he told his friend at the Hay Waggon that final afternoon. "The office employs him like a jailer."[90]

Suki Potier, Tom Keylock and Brian Jones

---

[89] Ibid p. 192
[90] Fitzgerald, p. 13

And Jones' jailkeeper came under enhanced scrutiny in 2009, when road manager Sam Cutler went public with what he'd learned from several discussions with financial manager Allen Klein. Klein did not trust the police and hired a team of private detectives to conduct an independent investigation into Jones' death. "Tom Keylock was the prime (and only) suspect named in that report," Cutler wrote in his blog.

"Brian Jones was murdered. Of this there is little doubt. He was not murdered by the man who was in charge of the building work at Brian's farm, a gentleman by the name of Thorogood who is popularly credited by conspiracy theorists with doing the deed. He was almost certainly murdered by the very man whose role it was to protect him, Tom Keylock. The man who less than forty-eight hours after the murder, emptied the house of its valuable contents, and burnt substantial amounts of papers and personal items of Brian Jones on a bonfire in the front garden."[91]

"On the night that Brian died Keylock always maintained that he was NOT at the farm. This was not true. He was at the farm. Not only was he at the farm, he was also in the swimming pool. Two witnesses testified to this to private investigators sent by Allen Klein. Allen Klein investigated the murder of Brian Jones, had private detectives go to a Nordic country and to France to interview two female witnesses, and it was the conclusion of the investigators that Keylock was directly responsible for Brian's death."

[Note: The only two possible female witnesses are Anna Wohlin, who was in Sweden, and Janet Lawson, who was hiding at her brother's RAF base in England. ZouZou, a close friend of Brian's since 1965, was probably the woman in France.]

"On the night Brian died there were several men in the pool with him. One was Frank Thorogood, the friend of Tom Keylock, whom Keylock had hired to do building work at Brian's house. Along with Thorogood there were two building workers who were employed by Thorogood. All three men were staying at the farm at Brian's expense. Then there was Keylock. A witness who arrived at Brian's farm while the events were in progress, describes a man holding down Brian's head under the water in the investigator's report. The witness (not one of the two women at the farm) was approached by a man (not

---

[91] Wecht, pp. 161-162

Keylock) who threatened him and he and his girlfriend who were personal friends of Brian's left the scene as quickly as possible. They immediately fled overseas and were never sought out by the British police."

[Note: The two building workers in the pool with Thorogood were Mo Tucker and Johnny Betsworth. Klein's detectives evidently caught up with Nicholas Fitzgerald long before he published his book. Not only did Fitzgerald possibly invent the claim that it was Keylock who discovered him watching from the bushes that night (it may have been somebody else). Fitzgerald had apparently gone to the Cotchford estate with his girlfriend Sara, not Richard Cadbury.]

"Neither of the female witnesses to the events which led to Brian's death were prepared to come to the United Kingdom and testify. Both witnesses (female) stated that they had been threatened and felt that their lives were in danger. Both witnesses testified [i.e. stated] that Keylock had been present in the swimming pool on the night and it was only many years after the event that **Keylock finally admitted to journalists that he had been on the scene,** *though he denied being in the pool or anywhere near the pool.* **Two men who had worked on the farm, and who were also present at the pool that evening, were never located or interviewed by the police.**

Conveniently (for Keylock) and several years after Brian's death, Frank Thorogood became so ill that he had to be hospitalized, he was a very sick man. Thorogood had been a witness to Brian's murder and had been in a business relationship with Keylock. Keylock had arranged for Thorogood and two other men to do the building work at Brian's farm. With Thorogood dying in the hospital Keylock visited him, and miraculously a 'death bed confession' was forthcoming, where (according to Keylock- the only witness) Thorogood admitted to "murdering Brian". This 'confession' had the convenient effect of diverting attention away from Keylock (who may well have felt under pressure from Klein's earlier inquiries) and placing it squarely upon Thorogood.

And there the matter rests. **It is believed the police in the United Kingdom now have copies of the Klein report.** *Klein was the manager of both the Rolling Stones and the Beatles and was determined to establish the cause of Brian's death- unlike the police who basically didn't give a damn. One can only assume that the Beatles and the Stones were privy to the conclusions* *of the Klein report, though no one has ever mentioned the existence of such a report. It is unknown whether the Klein report was ever given to the British police,* **but it is known that the police made no attempt to contact any of the witnesses named in the report.**"[92]

It does not seem that the Klein report was ever intended to be submitted to police; they may have simply seized it. Regardless of whether such a report ever even existed and was subsequently sealed or destroyed, Cutler's information revealed that: private detectives had tracked down eyewitnesses who placed Keylock, Thorogood and two builders at the pool area; Keylock himself may have been right in the pool; and police did not properly investigate the circumstances of Jones' death.

Keylock, as mentioned previously, finally admitted in 2009 that "of course I was there, where else would I have been? I had a job to do and I did it." His habitual alibi was that he'd spent the afternoon of July 2nd with Keith Richards, and had taken him to Olympic Studios in London early that evening. Richards then realized he'd forgotten a particular guitar he needed for that night's recording session, and asked Keylock to drive an hour and a half back to Redlands to fetch it. And on the return journey Keylock stopped in for a late-night dinner at "some sort of country club" he didn't remember the name of.

---

[92] http://samcutler.tumblr.com

It is more than curious that Keylock's alibi- later admitted to be fraudulent- could only have been corroborated by Keith Richards.

The question is: did he ever even leave Cotchford that night? A Sussex police drugs officer wrote in his notebook, about 12:30 AM: "When I entered the premises I saw two women, Frank Thorogood and a man with heavy glasses standing together in the kitchen, nervously talking and drinking tea."[93] *Allegedly*, he was seen about then at Olympic Studios by music writer Keith Altham: "I had got to Olympic around eleven on my way home; he came in about midnight, or one o'clock."[94] *But nobody else ever mentioned seeing Keylock arrive*, and pianist Ian Stewart took the call informing the band of Brian's death at 1:10 AM. And Stewart told the caller, who was Keylock's wife Joan, that Tom had not arrived.[95]

Keylock, in fact, eventually admitted on camera that he never left the premises that night. What he apparently did was instigate a series of phone calls that initiated a search to help find Tom Keylock- he was the Stones' fixer who could head out to Cotchford and keep a lid on this holy mess. And Keylock, of course, was at Cotchford the whole time, knowing a search to help track him down would also help establish his whereabouts as elsewhere.

Frank Thorogood first called Joan Keylock to tell her about Brian's death and ask her if she could get in touch with Tom. Joan proceeded to contact the Stones' secretary Shirley Arnold, relaying the news and asking to get a hold of her husband. Joan then phoned Olympic and broke the tragic news.

Allegedly, Keylock left Olympic Studios at approximately 2:30 AM and drove out to Cotchford with Stones publicist Les Perrin. *But there is no indication that Perrin was ever queried about this.* He seems to have been willing to turn a blind eye for the benefit of the organization. On

---

[93] Rawlings, p. 186

[94] Trynka, p. 334

[95] Rawlings, p. 150

July 6th Perrin would summon Anna Wohlin to his office to get her to sign an agreement forbidding her release of any information harmful to either Brian Jones or the Rolling Stones. Perrin would get copy-approval of anything she said in any interviews.[96]

Tom Keylock had an enabler who fueled his audacity on the night of July 2nd, and allowed him to literally get away with murder. His younger brother Frank was a senior investigator for Scotland Yard. He was a drinking buddy of Thorogood[97] and had the clout in the corrupt English police service to squelch any murder inquiries. Brian Jones was hated by the establishment anyways and, as much as anyone, personified the rebellious 60s and its cultural schism. He would not be missed.

There are indications that Frank Keylock may even have had advance knowledge of the rock star's death. Two newspaper reporters based in Brighton- 45 minutes away- were already at the Cotchford scene with the ambulance when PC Albert Evans arrived at 12:15 AM. They had been tipped off by Sussex drugs officer Mickey Dann, who was a protégé of Frank Keylock. Since the emergency call went out to the local police station at 12:10 AM, Dann was apparently notified of Brian Jones' death a half hour before it happened. Officially happened.

Evans noted, "There were many people there- more than a dozen or so before the Sussex CID officers arrived, all coming to look at the body beside the pool." Soon there seemed to be an overflow of police, called in from parts unknown. "There were other officers there but I don't know what they were doing."[98]

The newspaper reporters took pictures of the dead body, but these were confiscated by police.

The two highest-ranking officers to visit Cotchford that night were DCI Robert Marshall and Detective Sergeant Peter Hunter. But these were the ranks assigned to investigate non-suspicious deaths. Whenever a suspected homicide occurred it would be given to a Detective Superintendent from Scotland Yard. It had already been determined, in the early morning

[96] Wohlin, pp. 215-217
[97] Rawlings, p. 189
[98] Ibid p. 186

hours of July 3rd, that the death of Brian Jones was going to be a "death by misadventure"[99]

Wohlin and Lawson evading reporters on the morning of July 3rd

It is natural to assume that the police are bastions of justice but unfortunately they can be dirty through and through, especially in Britain in 1969. The notorious Norman Pilcher, who led drug raids against Donovan, the Beatles, the Stones and Eric Clapton, was sentenced himself to four years for perjury in 1972. "My boss at the time, Vic Keleher, and the commander, Wally Virgo, were totally corrupt," he revealed many years later. "I saw Keleher handling thousands of pounds that probably never ended up where it was meant to be."[100]

Frank Keylock passed away in 1998. *Allegedly*, he told his brother Tom that Jones' death was covered up because of mistakes by local police. "I think the police wanted to make a manslaughter charge," Tom related, "but they were told to forget it. The only one who could have possibly been charged was Frank Thorogood, because he was the only one in the pool.

---

[99] Brian Jones Fan Club statement by Trevor Hobley, 12/31/05
[100] The Cop Who Busted the Beatles Now Wants to Legalize All Drugs by J.S. Rafaeli, VICE 1/26/21

But the police said 'Just forget it'. **The order came from the very top not to pursue it anymore**, and it was never pursued after that."[101]

He told Terry Rawlings in 2009: "I'm fed up with people coming up with all these stories that Princess Margaret and so and so was down there. She wasn't, and nor was Elvis. I was there and I knew who was there, I was the only one who didn't eat the hash cakes- the police didn't even know about them. They didn't even know what a hash cake was…"

"… I was told to forget it, it was dealt with! **It went right to the very top**."[102]

In the final analysis, it matters little whether it was combat veteran Tom Keylock or builder Frank Thorogood who ultimately deprived Brian Jones of further breath. They were strong men in early middle age and they easily overpowered him with the help of Mo Tucker and Johnny Betsworth. We can't say for certain, at this point, whether death was delivered in the swimming pool or a nearby animal trough.

But Keylock seems to have orchestrated this murder. Thorogood badly injured his wrist, an indication that Brian Jones fought for his life. And Janet Lawson was an accessory after the fact.

Detectives always look for means, motive and opportunity, but in Keylock's case, the motive is missing. What could he possibly have stood to gain from murdering Brian Jones? A couple of gold record plaques? "Keylock was unpleasant," Keith Altham noted, "but why would he have murdered Brian when Brian was the goose that kept laying the golden egg?"[103]

Indeed, Keylock had the means and opportunity to murder his "prisoner", and the family connections to take the coverup right to the top of British law enforcement. But it makes no sense that he would risk murder charges for trivial personal gain.

Keylock very likely was acting at the behest of somebody else, who wanted Brian Jones dead. And his reward would be forthcoming.

This case goes much deeper than Tom Keylock.

---

[101] Fresh evidence on the Rolling Stones' Brian Jones' 'murder' appears in new Netflix documentary by John Earls, NME 7/29/19

[102] Rawlings, p. 163

[103] Trynka, p. 334

SEVEN

DEATH BY MISADVENTURE ?

The body of Brian Jones was brought to the morgue at Queen Victoria Hospital in East Grinstead at approximately 6:00 AM on July 3rd. The autopsy was performed that same day by forensic pathologist Dr. Albert Sachs. This was well before any bruising would have started appearing, an indicator he perhaps had been in a struggle.

The English press that day blamed a possible asthma attack and quoted Tom Keylock how "it was particularly bad when there was a lot of pollen about." Brian had had extreme asthma since he was a young boy. But the autopsy findings did not support this possibility. Sachs noted that the bronchi contained "a few flakes of glairy mucus, but not the viscous adherent mucus associated with death due to an asthma attack."

Additionally, he remarked that "In death from an asthmatic attack lungs are light and bulky." Jones' respiratory passages were found to have "frothy fluid round nostrils… blood stained fluid in mouth [and] frothy blood stained fluid" in the lungs. His heavy, wet lungs were consistent with a death by drowning.

Based upon the autopsy evidence alone, it cannot be determined whether that drowning was accidental, or a fatal dunking at the hands of another.[104] The apparent cause, "immersion in fresh water", refers to swimming pool water, which is not the salt water of the ocean. But it does not rule out the possibility that the immersion was in the water of an animal trough.

---

[104] Wecht, p. 165

An urban legend that Jones had the same brain injuries as seen in "shaken baby syndrome" is not supported by the autopsy results. On the contrary, his brain showed the classical indications of drowning: congestion, accumulation of fluid, and "punctate hemorrhaging in white matter"- the pinpoint bleeding that occurs as the brain struggles to get more oxygen.[105]

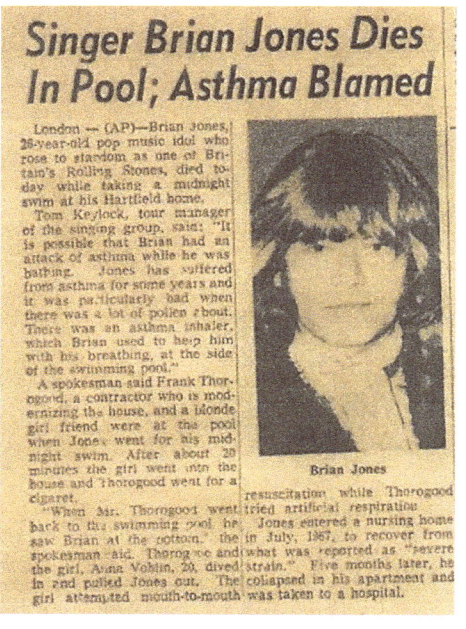

Singer Brian Jones Dies In Pool; Asthma Blamed

London — (AP)—Brian Jones, 26-year-old pop music idol who rose to stardom as one of Britain's Rolling Stones, died today while taking a midnight swim at his Hartfield home.

Tom Keylock, tour manager of the singing group, said: "It is possible that Brian had an attack of asthma while he was bathing. Jones has suffered from asthma for some years and it was particularly bad when there was a lot of pollen about. There was an asthma inhaler, which Brian used to help him with his breathing, at the side of the swimming pool."

A spokesman said Frank Thorogood, a contractor who is modernizing the house, and a blonde girl friend were at the pool when Jones went for his midnight swim. After about 20 minutes the girl went into the house and Thorogood went for a cigaret.

"When Mr. Thorogood went back to the swimming pool he saw Brian at the bottom," the spokesman said. Thorogood and the girl, Anna Vohlin, 20, dived in and pulled Jones out. The girl attempted mouth-to-mouth resuscitation while Thorogood tried artificial respiration.

Jones entered a nursing home in July, 1967, to recover from what was reported as "severe strain." Five months later, he collapsed in his apartment and was taken to a hospital.

Brian Jones

His blood alcohol level was 0.14, the equivalent of about seven whiskeys, or 3 ½ pints of beer. That is not particularly high for a chronic drinker like Brian Jones. It is more like a solid maintenance buzz, and not a level that would bring about more than a slight impairment of his normal functions. He was not driving anywhere.

Yet his body paid a price from years of drug and alcohol abuse. His liver weighed 3000 grams, about twice the normal adult size. It had lost its architecture and was overwhelmed with fatty deposits. Sachs was forced to admit that a contributing factor to Jones' premature death was "severe liver dysfunction due to fatty degeneration and ingestion of alcohol and drugs."

He sectioned liver and lung samples that afternoon and sent them to the coroner, Dr. Angus Sommerville, who was doubling as a pathologist in the histology department at the hospital. Sachs collected the small amount of urine that was retained and sent that along with a blood sample over to the Royal Sussex Hospital in Brighton for biochemical analysis.

Sommerville noted, under the microscope, that the linings of the lungs broke down in places and showed blistery patches (bullous areas). There was blood plasma (albuminoid material) in the lung sacs, as well

---

[105] Ibid p. 169

as hemorrhaging, which was consistent with the histology of drowning victims. And at the coroner's inquest on July 7th, he officially concluded that Brian Jones' death was due to "Drowning whilst under the influence of alcohol and drugs… <u>MISADVENTURE</u>." He topped that off with a personal moral admonition: "He would not listen. So he drowned under the influence of alcohol and drugs."[106]

---

[106] Trynka, p. 315

Notes of the Post-Mortem Examination of

Name of deceased Lewis Brian Jones.   Age 26   Sex Male

Address of deceased Cotchford Farm, Hartfield, Sussex.

Name of G.P.

Observers present at examination D.B.

Date and time of examination Mortuary, Queen Victoria Hospital

Place where examination performed E. Grinstead; 3rd July 1969.

Estimated time of death 11.30 - midnight 2nd July, 1969

Chief points in the history of the case.	Deceased apparently went for a swim in a pool at his home with friends. Friends left the pool and the deceased decided to stay in the water. Last seen alive 11.30 p.m. 2nd July, 1969. Found dead shortly afterwards.
EXTERNAL EXAMINATION Height(length), Weight	5' 9".
Apparent age	28 years of age.
Nourishment	Powerfully built; with a tendency to obesity.
Temperature at rectum	Not taken.
Rigor mortis, hypostasis, decomposition	Rigor mortis present. Hypostasis present.
Evidence of violence, burns	Nil.
Identification (tattoo marks, old scars, special deformities	Nil seen.
Body surface - Pallor, abnormal coloration	Pallor of face. Frothy fluid round nostrils.
Orifices of body, hair, teeth	Own teeth.
INTERNAL EXAMINATION Cranial Cavity Skull, scalp and face	N.A.D.
Brain - weight, etc.	Wt. 1553gms. Congested and oedematous. Punctate haemorrhages in white matter.
Meninges and blood vessels	Congested.
Spinal column, cord and meninges	N.A.D.
Thoracic Cavity Mouth, tongue, tonsils, oesophagus	Little blood stained fluid in mouth. Could be due to artificial respiration.
larynx, trachea, bronchi, thyroid and thymus glands	Respiratory tract. Mucosa congested. Bronchi contains a few flakes of glairy mucus, but this is not the viscid adherent mucus associated with death due to an asthmatic attack.
lungs, pleurae, diaphragm	Wt. L 632gms. R 643gms. Adhesions left base to chest wall. No free fluid to pleural cavities. Both lungs voluminous. Some areas of collapse. Lungs pit on pressure. Frothy blood stained fluid exudes from lungs on section. Few subpleural petechial
Pericardium	
Heart (size, weight, cavities and contents, valve orifices and cusps), heart muscle and coronary arteries	haemorrhages. Heart Wt. 411gms. General hypertrophy. Both sides dilated. Myocardium fatty and flabby. No evidence of vascular or valvular disease.

Brian Jones autopsy report

Aorta, pulmonary and other blood vessels	Blood from left side of heart showed 29% Mb plasma due to haemolysis. Aorta. Marrow but no Blood alcohol 140 mgs %
Internal injuries (thoracic)	Nil.
Abdominal Cavity Stomach and contents	About 10% of undigested food in fluid. Mucosa congested.
Peritoneum, intestines and contents, appendix, mesenteric glands, etc.	N.A.D.
Liver and gall bladder	Wt. 3000gms. Congested. Architecture lost. Sections show liver dysfunction due to extensive fatty degeneration. Gall bladder. Empty.
Spleen	Spleen Wt. 247gms. Congested.
Kidneys and ureters	Wt. L 190gms R 181gms. Congested.
Bladder and urine	Little urine present. Analysis showed 1720 micro-gms. % of a basic amphetamine-like substance.
Suprarenals, pancreas	Apparently normal.
Generative organs, breasts, prostate, etc.	Normal for age.
Internal injuries (abdominal)	Nil.
Are all other organs healthy?	Apparently.
Cause of death as shown by the examination :	In my opinion the cause of death was :-
Disease or condition directly leading to death * ... ... Antecedent causes ... ... Morbid conditions, if any, giving rise to the above cause stating the underlying condition last ...	(a) Drowning. due to (or as a consequence of) (b) Immersion in fresh water. due to (or as a consequence of) (c)
II	
Other significant conditions, contributing to the death, but not related to the disease or condition causing it ✎	Severe liver dysfunction due to fatty degeneration and the ingestion of alcohol and drugs.

* This does not mean the mode of dying, such as, e.g. heart failure, asphyxia, asthenia, etc., it means the disease, injury or complication which caused death.

✎ Conditions which do not in the pathologist's opinion contribute materially to the death should not be included under this heading.

These notes should be short and contain records of the facts observed; if opinions are expressed the grounds upon which they are based should also be stated. Scientific terms should be avoided when possible.

Any further remarks :
In death from an asthmatic attack lungs are light and bulky.

Signature and qualifications Albert Sachs, CB, CBE, MD, MSc. PROF. F. C .Path

Address Queen Victoria Hospital, E. Grinstead, Sussex.

Date 5th July, 1969

11/61

CLS/394/3070/2/0

Brian Jones autopsy report (continued)

Pathological Report No. 669 Date received: 3.7.69 HISTOLOGY
T QUEEN VICTORIA HOSPITAL. PM. Specimen Liver-frozen.
EAst GRINSTEAD. Ward: Site Lungs x 2.
Name: Brian Jones. Age:26 Surgeon or Physician: Dr. Somerville.

Lungs. The alveolar spaces are dilated and show bullous areas due to
breakdown of the alveolar septa. Albumin-id material is present
in the alveolar spaces. Subpleural haemorrhage is present. This
is the histology found in drowning.

Date: Signed: Pathologist.

Brian Jones histology report

It is notable that the coroner's official verdict included in its synopsis of preliminary circumstances that Jones was "Seen to stagger on the Diving Board before jumping off into the Swimming Pool." But this particular incident was only mentioned in Janet Lawson's police statement, which she later contended was a "pack of lies". It had actually been written up for her by Detective Sergeant Peter Hunter.

The biochemical toxicology analysis was performed by a "Mr. Cook" at the Royal Sussex Hospital. And it revealed a couple of suspicious affairs.

The first dealt with an *amphetamine-like* substance found in the urine. This weighed 1720 micrograms, almost nine times the normal metabolic residue, high enough to "suggest ingestion of a fairly large quantity of a drug." Brian had knowingly or unknowingly taken a sizeable dose of a nervous system stimulant on the day he died. Since it was in his urine at the time of death, the *amphetamine-like* substance was on its way out of his body. Whatever effect it had had on his brain had since passed. This particular drug did not contribute to his death,[107] although, we shall soon see, it may have been spiked into the steak and kidney pie.

---

[107] Wecht, p. 166

INQUISITION

123

An inquisition taken for our Sovereign Lady the Queen

At THE MAGISTRATES COURT In the PARISH of EAST GRINSTEAD SUSSEX.

On the SEVENTH day of JULY, . 1969

[And at such adjournments on the] 19 I

[Before and by] (1) me Angus Christopher SOMMERVILLE.

one of her Majesty's coroners for the said County of Sussex.

[and the undermentioned jurors] touching the death of (2) Lewis Brian JONES.

whose body has been viewed by me (3)

[containing EXHIBITS]

1. Name of deceased: Lewis Brian JONES.

2. Injury or disease causing death: (4)
   1 (a) Drowning
   (b) Immersion in Fresh Water.
   II. Severe liver dysfunction due to fatty degeneration and the ingestion of alcohol and drugs.

3. Time, place and circumstances at or in which injury was sustained: (5) Approximately 11.30 p.m., on the 2nd July, 1969, at Cotchford Farm, Hartfield, Sussex. Deceased had been drinking earlier in the evening, and was seen to be obviously under the influence of Alcohol and apparently Drugs. Insisted on going for a bathe. Seen to stagger on the Diving Board before jumping off into Swimming Pool, but managed to swim with other companion in Pool. Latter left to get Towel, returned to find deceased at bottom of Pool.

4. Conclusion of the jury/coroner as to the death:
Drowning whilst/under the influence of Alcohol and Drugs.
Swimming
MISADVENTURE.

5. Particulars for the time being required by the Registration Acts to be registered concerning the death :

(1) When and where died	(2) Name and surname of deceased	(3) Sex	(4) Age or probable age	(5) Occupation and address
11.30 p.m. 2nd July, 1969. Cotchford Farm, Hartfield, Sussex.	Lewis Brian JONES.	M	27	Entertainer, of Cotchford Farm, Hartfield, Sussex.

Signature of jurors: Signature of coroner:—

P.T.O.

Coroner's official verdict

Sudden Death — Brian JONES

The Deceased was under the care of Dr. A.L. GREENBURGH of 73 Eaton Place, Belgravia, W.1., telephone Belgravia 3232.

Dr. GREENBURGH was away in Majorca until the late evening of Sunday, 6th July. Was contacted at his surgery at 9.15 a.m. on Monday, 7th July.

The Doctor confirmed that the Deceased was regularly prescribed:

MANDREX — as sleeping tablets, 2 to 3 per day.

VALIUM — (10 mg) — as tranquillizers, 3 per day, which, 'he needed all of the time'.

MEDIHALER — regular prescriptions — Doctor has never been consulted by the Deceased for asthma.

DUROPHET — ("black bombers") infrequently.

PIRITON — 4 mg., was prescribed day before death as a result of a telephone call from Deceased, complaining of hay-fever.

About ten days ago, the Deceased made an urgent telephone call to Dr. GREENBURGH, requesting Durophet and a prescription for ten or so was given.

Dr. GREENBURGH stated that the Deceased's drug requirements were becoming less and he had shown considerable improvement of late. Prescriptions were made in small quantities at frequent intervals rather than large prescriptions, which, experience had shown, resulted in the Deceased taking larger doses.

[signature]

DC1.

7/7/69

Brian Jones' psychiatrist's report

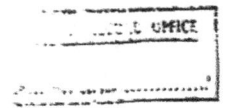

UNBRIDGE WELLS GROUP HOSPITAL MANAGEMENT COMMITTEE
THE QUEEN VICTORIA HOSPITAL
EAST GRINSTEAD, SUSSEX
PATRON
H.M. QUEEN ELIZABETH, THE QUEEN MOTHER
HONORARY PRESIDENT
GLADYS, LADY KINGERSLEY

PHONE : EAST GRINSTEAD 24111
TELEGRAMS : QVICHOS, EAST GRINSTEAD

PATHOLOGIST :
A. SACHS, C.B., C.B.E.
M.SC., M.D. ...., FRCP, F.C. Path.

PATHOLOGICAL LABORATORY   7th July, 1969.

Telephone report from Mr. Cook, Biochemist, Royal Sussex
Hospital, Brighton.

1.	**Blood barbiturate.**	Nil.
2.	**Blood alcohol.**	140mgs; (Approx 7 whiskeys, or 3¾ pints of beer)
3.	**Urine.**	Amphetamine like substance 1720 micro-gms. (in normal urine this never exceeds 200 micro gms.) These figures suggest ingestion of a fairly large quanity of a drug
4.	**Thin layer chromatography.**	Failed to reveal the presence of the following in an unchanged state.

      (a) Amphetamine.
      (b) Methedrine.
      (c) Morphine.
      (d) Methadrone.
      (e) Isoprenaline.

But did show the presence of 2 dense spots, one yellow
orange which has not been identified and the other a
purple spot. This could be due to diphenhydramine, which
is present together with methaqualone in Mandrax, which
the deceased is known to have taken.

Brian Jones toxicology report

The second dealt with two dense spots that turned up after thin-layer chromatography of the blood sample. One spot was yellow-orange and was not identified by Mr. Cook. Another spot was purple, and the possibility was raised that it "could be due to diphenhydramine, which is present together with methaqualone in Mandrax, which the deceased is known to have taken."

Mandrax is a powerful and addictive sedative, each tablet usually consisting of 250 mg of methaqualone and 25 mg of diphenhydramine. Brian had been taking them for years and was prescribed "2 or 3 per day" by his psychiatrist, Dr. A.L. Greenburgh. He was also prescribed

Valium tranquilizers on top of that, 3 per day, which "he needed all the time." Given his penchant for alcohol abuse, coupled with those powerful sedatives, Brian Jones was a runaway train fast running out of available track.

One might easily conclude that his substance abuse finally derailed him on the night of July 2nd. But that deduction ignores the critical piece of evidence pertaining to the circumstances of his death: the presence of Keylock, Tucker and Betsworth at the pool that night was suppressed. Not only did Brian's substance abuse make him an easier target for murder. As a contributing cause of death it fit his murderers' cloaks beautifully.

There is a good possibility that the yellow-orange spot in the chromatography assay was from tetrahydrocannibinol in the hash cakes. Investigators at that time in Britain would not have considered testing for it, which may have been the reason this prominent spot was unidentified.

The controls in this toxicology study all tested negative: amphetamine and Methadrine (i.e. methamphetamine), morphine and methadone (both opiods) and isoprenaline (the asthma drug ingredient that dilates bronchial tubes). None of them were in his bloodstream and since they can take a couple of days to completely metabolize, it is unlikely they were even taken by Brian that day.

It was a sin of omission not to test him for Mandrax (methaqualone) or Valium (diazepam). An extra dosage, particularly in conjunction with alcohol, would have led to dangerous impairment. His psychiatrist was contacted by the autopsist on the afternoon of the 4th, and relayed the prescription information. This should have been forwarded to the biochemist for the toxicology analysis, but it wasn't. As it stood, they had no way of knowing whether these prescriptions contributed to his death- a rather obvious potential clue. Dr. Greenburgh did testify at the July 7th inquest that Brian's "drug requirements were becoming less and he had shown considerable improvement of late."

Greenburgh also stated that Brian had made an emergency request for some Durophet about ten days prior to his death. This powerful stimulant is a mixture of amphetamine and dexedrine (dextroamphetamine), known by its street name as "black bombers". He was provided a prescription for "ten or so".

Curiously enough, drugs officer Michael Harvey found a packet with five black capsules in the breast pocket of a suitcoat during his search of the living room. Shortly after dawn, when Frank Thorogood returned from the police station, he acknowledged that the sportsjacket belonged to him.

"These capsules appear to be Durophet, which is a restricted drug," Harvey pointed out. "Did you obtain them lawfully?"

"They are Brian's," Thorogood conceded.

"What have you got them in your possession for then?"

"I look after them for Brian so that he won't take too many at a time."

Statement of Witness
(C.J. Act, 1967, ss 2,9, M.C. Rules 1967, r. 7.)

Name __Michael Anthony Harvey__

Occupation of Witness __Police Constable AH 258__

Address __Sussex Drugs Squad, Malling House, Lewes, Sussex.__

Telephone No. __Lewes 5432 Ext.273.__   Age __Over 21__
(if over 21 enter 'over 21')

At 3.am on Thursday 3rd July 1969, I was on duty in plain clothes accompanied by PC Bureham, at Crotchford Farm, Hartfield, Sussex. I was assisting local Police officers, enquiring into the death of a well known 'pop' singer.

At the time, I was making a search of the premises in order that any evidence may be obtained to assist the Coroner, in deciding the cause of death. In the living room of the premises, I saw a coat hanging on a hook on the wall. I searched the coat, and in the top breast pocket found a cut envelope, with the words 'SUEBOARD' thereon.

I examined this envelope and saw that it contained five black capsules. I made enquires and found that the jacket belonged to the defendant Francis David THOROGOOD. At this time THOROGOOD was at East Grinstead Police Station, helping Police officers with their enquiries into the death of the pop singer. I remained on the premises until 8am the same day when THOROGOOD returned to the farm.

After telling him who I was, I said to him, "Is this your jacket?" indicating the jacket in which I had found the black capsules. He replied, "Yes." I then said, "While searching this room for evidence relating to the death of Mr. Jones, I searched your jacket and found something." I then went to get the capsules out of the pocket. As I did so, THOROGOOD said, "Yes, I know what you found." I then showed the black capsules to him and said, "These capsules appear to be durophet, which is a restricted drug. Did you obtain them lawfully?" He replied, "They are Brian's." I then said, "What have you got them in your possession for then?" I cautioned him, and he replied, "I look after them for Brian so that he won't take too many at a time." I then

Signature of Witness _____

Michael Harvey's police report

64

Form G.12/3   6   Page 240

Cont'd/

said. "In that case you must be in unlawful possession of them." He replied, "Yes I suppose so." I then said, "The capsules will be sent away for analysis. If they are found to be a restricted substance it will be necessary for me to see you again." He replied, "Oh, right then."

The capsules which I had found in possession of this woman were sealed and packaged by me and sent by recorded delivery to the Metropolitan Police Forensic Science Laboratory, Holborn, London W.C.1.

[signature]

Continued

This statement, consisting of _____ pages each signed by me is true to the best of my knowledge and belief and I make it knowing that, if it is tendered in evidence I shall be liable to prosecution if I have wilfully stated in it anything which I know to be false or do not believe to be true.

Signature *Harvey* PA8 228

Dated this 5th day of July 1969

The above statement was taken by me at _____ am/pm _____ at (place)

in the presence of _____

and signed by the maker after he/she had read it over/I had read it over to him/her and he/she had been invited to make any additions or alterations thereto.

Signature of Officer taking statement

"In that case you must be in unlawful possession of them." "Yes, I suppose so."

"The capsules will be sent away for analysis," Harvey warned. "If they are found to be a restricted drug it will be necessary for me to see you again."

"Oh, right then."

And they were subsequently delivered to the Metropolitan Police Lab in London. Michael Harvey concluded his report with "Cautioned", handwritten and underlined, underneath his signature.

But these lab results disappeared and Thorogood never faced any criminal charges, which would normally have been the case. Harvey was tracked down in 2008 by journalist Scott Jones and dodgily responded that "given the circumstances, it didn't justify court proceedings. That was a decision made by a senior officer." That person would have been DCI Robert Marshall, but he claimed to have no knowledge that Durophet had been found at the estate. Yet Marshall had also met with Harvey's superior that morning, Chief Constable T.C. Williams, who "knew Brian Jones was dead and we'd found some drugs in there."

"Chief Constables were and still are political animals," explained an anonymous local officer familiar with the case. "If the Chief Constable knew drugs had been found in the house you'd expect him to say, 'I want the man charged'."

A caution wouldn't be written onto a report "unless you knew the Chief Constable was backing you. It was decided this information about the drugs find would not be given to the coroner. It's outrageous."[108]

Indeed, Harvey's official police report, submitted on July 5th, was not included at the coroner's inquest two days later.

With Janet Lawson's claim that she witnessed Thorogood spiking the steak & kidney pie that afternoon, and Thorogood found to be in possession of Brian's Durophet, it is natural to speculate that perhaps the pie was laced with a few black bombers. This is a bizarre choice, given that- if the idea was to incapacitate Brian- this drug had the opposite effect. Yet if Mandrax had been used instead, it would have had a more pronounced effect on the slightly-built Anna Wohlin. It is questionable whether she

---

[108] Has the riddle of Rolling Stones Brian Jones' death been solved at last? by Scott Jones, Daily Mail 11/29/08

would even have roused from her stupor, which set in after she had gone upstairs to take a phone call. Her temporary drowsiness was likely caused by the hash cakes.

Wohlin and Thorogood arriving at inquest

Yet considering that Thorogood was habitually intoxicated, he may have selected the black capsules out of sheer ignorance. He wouldn't have known that the amphetamine mixture boils away at 400 degrees, a typical baking temperature. And its degraded, *amphetamine-like* residue- which had little to no effect on Brian Jones' metabolism- is what was found clustered in his urine.

This idea receives some corroboration from a 2009 forensic analysis of the fireplace in the music room commissioned by Trevor Hobley. That search for some trace of a chemical residue which might have incapacitated Jones came up negative. The truth is that Brian was in reasonable possession of his faculties that night. It took four strong men to subdue him, and one of them injured his wrist. This event would have greater chances for success outside of Brian's element, the swimming pool, where he had notable prowess.

According to the people that knew him best, Brian Jones was steering clear of his notorious proclivity for drug abuse while at Cotchford. His move to the country helped ease the stresses of London and its music scene excesses. He still had a lingering paranoia from his sensationalized drug busts and would not allow marijuana to be smoked at his farmhouse.

"I'm clean now, I'm a boozer again," he explained to Stones photographer Tony Sanchez, "Spanish Tony", who offered some cocaine during a visit to the estate.[109]

Jones had settled on a routine of vodka or brandy, mingled in with a steady dependence on prescription drugs. "He had been drinking every minute of the day," Anna Wohlin recalled, "without seeming at all drunk and it was then that I realized what everyone had been saying was true. He was an alcoholic."[110] But she never saw him use any drugs, apart from Mandrax or Valium, while she was living with him.[111]

"He was still drinking a lot and at one point fell asleep in mid-sentence," said Alexis Korner, who visited many times that June. Brian also frequented the Hay Waggon pub and one night crashed his motor scooter into a nearby shop window.[112]

He had never taken heroin.[113] This was despite being in the company of noted abusers Keith Richards and Mick Jagger, along with their girlfriends Anita Pallenberg and Marianne Faithfull- who consumed some of the choicest cuts that money could buy. Jones somehow realized that his own insatiable appetite would have led to an overdose.

"He was never into heavy drugs," Pallenberg said. "Just alcohol and pills. By then [his premature death] he'd also stopped taking acid… I do know he was never into heroin- in fact, wasn't even smoking- because apart from everything else he was too paranoiac…"

"… he was very creative again. Alexis Korner had gotten in touch with him, and they were going to form another band, a blues band.

[109] Rawlings, p. 101
[110] Ibid p. 108
[111] Wohlin, pp. 127-132
[112] Rawlings, pp. 102-103
[113] Fitzgerald, p. 252

He had regained his vision, but physically he was still recovering. And John Lennon was also talking to him about forming a band. Apart from anything else they both had this same kind of 'up-front thing'. So basically, I think he was in a lot better shape by then... That's what's so sad and frankly still quite suspicious about his death."[114]

The virtually same-day autopsy only compounded those suspicions. No time given for any bruises to manifest. No blood analysis for Mandrax or Valium. No sign of amphetamine in the blood- yet a high concentration of an amphetamine-like residue in the urine. Durophet, had it been swallowed as usual would have shown some signs of metabolizing- yet this residue was a suspicious indication that someone had attempted to spike Brian Jones. And the police discovery of his Durophet in that someone's hands was suppressed.

His body was embalmed and his hair was bleached white, probably at the request of his parents. It was sealed in an airtight silver and bronze casket. To discourage trophy hunters, it was buried 12 feet deep in St. Mary's Churchyard in his hometown of Cheltenham. Only a week after his death the autopsy, inquest and burial were all said and done.

---

[114] The Early Stones by Terry Southern, Hyperion (1992)

Notable forensic pathologist Cyril Wecht, a leading medical expert on JFK's death, criticized the documentation surrounding Jones' death as "atypically brief... the biggest problem with the autopsy is its lack of detail."[115] In 1994 a consultant pathologist for the Home Office, Dr. C.M. Milroy, examined the records of Jones' autopsy and inquest and concluded he "cannot exclude the possibility that Jones was held under water."[116]

The coroner from neighboring East Sussex, Dr. David Wadman, indicated that Jones' death was investigated by the Home Office.[117] This is a British parliamentary department- responsible for security, immigration, and law and order- and it has its own Cabinet minister. This is what Keylock was referring to when he said that the coverup went "right to the very top".

This circumstance better explains why the Sussex coroner, Angus Sommerville, received a substantial amount of shares in Dunlop tire the same day he took charge of Jones' body.[118] This was no coincidence. Sommerville had nothing but speculation to back up his verdict that Jones had drowned whilst under the influence of drugs and alcohol. It was politically expedient to dismiss this troublemaker with his pronouncement of death by misadventure. And the coroner thereby became a key accessory after the fact in Brian Jones' murder.

---

[115] Wecht, pp. 163, 167
[116] Rawlings, p. 221
[117] Rawlings, p. 154
[118] Ibid pp. 190, 234

Scott Jones was interviewed extensively for the 2019 film documentary *Rolling Stone: Life and Death of Brian Jones*. And in it he stated that, "I've had the medical reports analysed by senior Home Office pathologists. And they have said that the stress on the tissues around the heart show that- Brian Jones would have been where- he was being murdered. Apparently the body responds in a certain way and they can tell- through the tissue damage- what level of stress the body was under…"

"… There was a trough in the garden. And that trough contained water. It would have been fresh water. It could easily have been the case that Brian actually died outside of the swimming pool… That was the water that was inside his lungs. It wasn't chlorinated water. There were no chemicals inside the lungs."[119]

There was corroboration for this given by recording artist Roxanne Fontana. As a star-obsessed teenager in 1974, she had created the International Brian Jones Memorial Fan Club in her hometown of New York. Twenty years later she began making trips to the Cotchford Farm estate and became acquainted with Mary and Les Hallett. These continued after Mary passed away.

In the film documentary, Fontana related that "the last time I saw Les Hallett- it was just hello, how are you? And then as I was leaving the area- leaving the property of Cotchford and going down the drive- he was running after my car, saying, 'They drowned him in the trough! They drowned him in the trough!'

And I didn't- what's a trough? Right? So I guess it's a barrel of some sort, but- he said, 'They drowned him in the trough and they threw him in the pool'!"

Fontana's revelation contradicts Trevor Hobley's information, that the Halletts hadn't woken up until about midnight- so they hadn't really heard any girls screaming or cars screeching away around 10:00 PM. Hobley had recorded his interviews with the couple when both were alive. This disclosure would also push back Nicholas Fitzgerald's story about spying on five people gathered around the swimming pool. That would have occurred closer to ten, which makes good sense, since he'd gone off to a nearby hotel about seven.

---

[119] Rolling Stone: Life and Death of Brian Jones by Danny Garcia (2019)

"The neighbor was adamant that he was drowned in the trough," filmmaker Danny Garcia maintained.[120] It would appear that Les Hallett was no longer fearful about whatever repercussions might come from speaking the truth. Luck would have it that this went out to a lifelong fan of Brian Jones, who had been inspired to make a career for herself in the music business.

The coroner must have known all along that a trough- or some outdoor receptacle for water, other than a swimming pool- had been the place where Brian Jones was drowned. When he looked at the lung sample he found traces of algae, according to a 2022 claim that surfaced on Facebook.

[120] The Life of Brian Jones Redeemed in a New Film Alleging his Murder by J. Morehead, LA Weekly, 1/11/20

EIGHT

ANITA PALLENBERG

Anita Pallenberg was a precocious Italian blonde of German and Swedish blood. She grew up in Rome and spoke five languages, played the cello and won a scholarship to the prestigious Academia di Belle Arti di Roma. But she preferred the intensity of trendsetting globetrotters and by age nineteen was modeling in Paris for the exclusive Catherine Hardé agency. Its roster included ZouZou and eventually added others who would also become a part of the Rolling Stones' camp- Marianne Faithfull, Nico and Talitha Getty.

"Anita was beautiful, but she was very dangerous company," recalled French author Fabrice Gaignault. "When you were close to her, you didn't know what was going to happen... All the men were crazy about her, but they were afraid of what she could do."

"She had a fantastic aura about her, very seductive power," added model Deborah Dixon. "And she was funny. She was well read, well travelled and with a great sense of adventure and curiosity. Anita had a cat-like grace and a wonderful laugh."[121]

"How Anita came to be with Brian, is really the story of how the Stones became the Stones," said Marianne Faithfull. "She almost single-handedly engineered a cultural revolution in London by bringing together the Stones and the *jeunesse dorée*[122] - the gilded youth, of wealth and fashion.

---

[121] She's a Rainbow: The Extraordinary Life of Anita Pallenberg by Simon Wells, Omnibus Press, London (2020) pp. 21-22

[122] Faithfull: An Autobiography by Marianne Faithfull, Cooper Square Press, New York (1994) p. 60

Pallenberg first saw the Stones perform in Paris in April of 1965. She attended that concert with a mutual friend of Brian Jones- "Stash", a percussionist and artist whose full name was Prince Stanislaw Klossowski de Rola. During the show she turned to the singer Françoise Hardy and told her, while espying Brian, "Give me four months and I'll be with that guy."

In a Munich auditorium that September her wish came true. While the band was rendering their smash hit *(I Can't Get No) Satisfaction*, Jones took impish delight in underweaving the theme song from *Popeye the Sailorman*. Mick Jagger soon began goose-stepping around the stage and set off a riot that police had to quell with a water cannon.[123] Anita snuck backstage and went straight for Brian. He told her he was "the leader of the group."[124]

"Brian was very well spoken, soft spoken, spoke German as well," Pallenberg recalled. "He captivated me with the way he moved, his hair, his soft manner. He wanted to capture your attention when he was speaking. He was sensitive, highly strung, totally ahead of his time, and also part of *another* time. The dandy with his clothes and all of that!"

She offered him a joint to smoke and subsequently he invited her back to his hotel room. There he unloaded that "he was so upset with Mick and Keith… they had teamed up on him… He was so vulnerable. Brian had everything going for him, I felt so sorry for him… I spent all night holding him while he cried."[125]

Pallenberg moved right into Jones' Chelsea Mews apartment and they quickly became Swinging London's first alpha couple. They were only 23 and the renaissance world was their oyster. They hosted Dylan, the Byrds and a mecca of artists, models and photographers of the new bohemian aristocracy. And proceeded to indulge in an excess of psychedelic drugs and a

[123] Fitzgerald, pp. 174-175
[124] Faithfull, p. 61
[125] Wells, pp. 35-36

highly-charged sexuality that could intimidate others around them. "The wedding is definitely on," Jones told the *New Musical Express*. "And Bob Dylan will be best man."[126]

"They were so sexually stimulated they could hardly leave the room before starting to shag," Peter Townshend recalled. "I thought Brian was living on a higher plane of decadence than anyone I would ever meet."[127]

"When I met Anita," said Stones manager Andrew Loog Oldham, "I did recognize a force, a power that would affect not just Brian, but the path of the Rolling Stones... whatever the upcoming chapters were to be for the Stones, Anita would be one of its main writers."[128]

She began coaxing Jones to dress up in silk blouses, scarves, velvet suits, hats, boots and bracelets- outright women's clothing that blurred the customary boundaries and brought bling to his presence. Anita Pallenberg thereby instigated an elegant bohemian androgyny that spilled over to the other members of the Rolling Stones. And she left an indelible mark on Brian Jones' legacy. Not only was he rock 'n roll's finest multi-instrumentalist. His trailblazing fashion sense and snappy stage appearance revolutionized the rock show and was only matched by his good friend Jimi Hendrix.

---

[126] Ibid p. 42
[127] Trynka, p. 169
[128] Wells, p. 38

"She was definitely in control of that relationship," Patti Boyd remembered. "You could see that she could do exactly what she wanted… She had such charisma and confidence… She was actually a bit scary. To me, it seemed that she had secrets that she would never reveal."[129]

"They were beautiful, they were the spitting image of each other and not an ounce of modesty existed between the two of them," added Marianne Faithfull, who would watch them dress. "I would sit mesmerized for hours, watching them preening in the mirror trying on each other's clothes. All rules and gender would evaporate in the narcissistic performance."[130]

But there was trouble in paradise and the tempest was unleashed both ways. Anita was a fiery Italian girl and was known to slap another woman competing for Brian's affection. She was once witnessed bashing him and

[129] Ibid p. 45
[130] Faithfull, p. 61

knocking him down when they'd arrived at a party. And Brian made a habit of hitting her.

"One day I arrived at his place in Chelsea to find Anita with bruises all over her face," Tony Sanchez related. "It was obvious he had beaten her savagely. When I asked her what had happened, she said, 'It's none of your business'."

After one episode, while recuperating at a friend's, she made a wax effigy of Brian and poked it with a needle and "...said whatever words I said and closed my eyes and jabbed the needle... It pierced the stomach... Next morning... I found him suffering from severe stomach pains. He'd been up all night, and he was in agony, bottles of milk of magnesia and other medications all around him. It took him a day or two to get over it."[131]

Another incident flared up in June of 1966, while on a holiday in Marbella, Spain. During a restaurant stop they began shouting insults and trading punches, throwing glasses at each other and overturning tables. Brian was taken away by police and Anita was soon arrested attempting to steal a car.

This was topped that August while on a trip to Tangier. "They fought about everything- cars, prices, restaurant menus," recalled Christopher Gibbs. "Brian could never win an argument with Anita, although he always made the mistake of trying. There would be terrible scenes of them screaming with each other. The difference was that Brian didn't know what he was doing. Anita did know what she was doing. I think that in a more gracious age, Anita would have been called a witch."[132]

In their room at the El Minzak Brian swung furiously at Anita. But he missed and hit a metal window frame and fractured his wrist. He spent a week in the hospital but recovered in time for the Stones' September tour of the UK.

---

[131] Wells, p. 50
[132] Wells, pp. 64-66

The volatile couple moved into an apartment on Courtfield Road, which they transposed into "a veritable witches' coven of decadent illuminati, rich princelings and hip aristos."[133] Faithfull, with a newborn baby and a dissolving marriage, began using it as a crash pad.

So did Keith Richards, who was depressed over a breakup with his girlfriend, Linda Keith. He would walk the four miles every day from an extra apartment he used in St. John's Wood.[134]

The trio bonded not only from shopping expeditions to clothing and antiques stores, but endless LSD trips together. This was a period when Mick Jagger admitted to using psychedelics "every day for a year."[135]

---

[133] Faithfull, p. 58

[134] Ibid p. 63

[135] 'I got Mick Jagger to quit heroin… but I could never get him to give up GIRLS': Jerry Hall reveals in long-awaited biography by Jo McFarlane, Daily Mail 9/25/10

There were seances using a Ouija board and middle of the night excursions to look for UFOs. A local esoteric bookstore, Indica, fueled their passion for arcane knowledge and unorthodox teachings.

"It was all very intellectual," Pallenberg later stated. "I read the entire works of Madame Blavatsky, the Tibetan-influenced theosophist, in a week. We'd all pass those books around. It wasn't all drugs and hedonism."

Tara Browne would regularly drop by, since he shared the avante-garde couple's interest in the occult. He and Jones each believed their lives would end prematurely.[136] Brian started to paint the mural of a graveyard on the wall behind his bed, with a blank headstone for his pillow.[137]

After Browne died that December, Brian, Anita, Keith and his old flame Linda holed up for the Christmas holidays in the George V hotel in Paris. They were distraught and drowned their sorrows with prodigious amounts of cocaine, amphetamines and powerful barbituates.

Anita had just finished her first film, ***Mord und Totschlag*** titled ***A Degree of Murder*** for anglo audiences, although it translated literally to "blood and thunder". She was nominated for the best actress at the German film awards, but the film's X-rating gave it a 10-year delay in reaching its target youth market, and it remains relatively unknown.

Brian composed the soundtrack, playing guitar, sitar, Mellotron, harmonica, dulcimer and autoharp. He enlisted the support of guitarist Jimmy Page, pianist Nicky Hopkins and Small Faces drummer Kenny Jones. Despite the initial marvelous reviews, the quantity of prepared material was lacking, and a soundtrack was never released. The master tapes were relegated to a producer's basement and were inadvertently thrown away.[138]

As Brian was finishing up the soundtrack in February, Mick and Keith got busted at the Redlands estate in a raid that became a sensationalized trial a few months later. To escape the attendant stresses, the Courtland Road trio decided to take a holiday in Morocco and meet up with some of their other London friends. They embarked in Richards' sumptuous Bentley Continental, chauffeured by hard-man Tom Keylock.

---

[136] Wells, pp. 70-72

[137] Faithfull, p. 68

[138] Brian Jones: A Degree of Murder by Richie Unterberger, Please Kill Me, 2/17/20

On their way down through France Brian developed respiratory problems and had to be hospitalized in Toulouse. He was diagnosed with pneumonia. They proceeded on without him and, as Richards explained it, "somewhere between Barcelona and Valencia, Anita and I looked at each other, and the tension was so high in the back seat, the next thing I know she's giving me a blow job."[139]

Jones, Pallenberg and Richards simmering at a Marrakech café

---

[139] Wells, p. 99

A couple of weeks later Brian, Keith and Anita- joined now by Mick-had reunited in Tangier. They made their way down to the opulent El Saadi hotel in Marrakech. "No sooner had we checked into our room," Anita stated, "than Brian began to berate me and attack me physically, beating me with a sobbing frustration."

"Brian started drinking, getting himself into a state," Keylock recounted. "Next thing anyone knew was that he'd picked up this pair of dodgy Berber whores, tattooed all over."[140]

Anita refused to participate in Brian's intended *ménage à quatre*. In his ensuing rage, she broke two of his ribs and a finger. "He overturned a tray full of sandwiches and cold cuts," she said, "spilling them all over the carpet. And then he began to pick things up and throw them at me."[141]

She ran for the safety of Keith and a plan was immediately hatched to flee the country before the meltdown escalated further. Using a ruse that tabloid reporters had just arrived in town, Keylock whisked Jones away from view into a marketplace with a longtime friend, the painter Bryan Gysin.

"The Stones are strong and the Stones will win, but we do have a weak link. You know who it is- Brian. He talks his bloody head off to reporters and tells them everything. Brian must be kept away from them for his own good and ours."[142] Meanwhile the remainder of the Stones party hightailed it back to London.

"He phoned me. He couldn't believe what had happened," Stash recounted. "What had occurred... they didn't confront him. Keith never stood up to Brian and said, 'You motherfucker'. He didn't say a word. He just decided to leave. That was what Brian was the most shocked by- the way he was simply abandoned. No money. Just stuck in a hotel, on his own."[143]

"Brian loved Mick and Keith. He really did," said Linda Lawrence, who bore his second son in 1964. "He considered them brothers. This was like having your own family reject you."

---

[140] Ibid pp. 105, 108
[141] Wells, p. 109
[142] Rawlings, p. 77
[143] Trynka. P. 228

"Brian was completely head over heels in love with Anita. He was badly betrayed," recalled Les Perrin's wife Jane. "What Keith and Anita did to Brian was the dirtiest thing of all."[144]

"First they took my music," Jones lamented. "Then they took my band. And now they've taken my love."

"I'd already made the decision about him before the trip to Africa," Pallenberg later admitted. "I'd already been enchanted and swept up by Keith. Brian knew that."[145]

Thus began a relationship with Richards that stretched over a dozen years, produced three children, and saw her immersed deeper into the occult and an addiction to heroin.

To prevent Jones from leaving the band, she made a false promise that she would reconcile with him after their upcoming spring tour of Europe. She soon began rehearsals for her second movie role, the Black Queen, in the campy science-fiction flick **Barbarella**. She lived it night and day and "got lost in the part… Anita was just getting into her part more than some might consider sane," Faithfull related. "But I don't think it can be simply written off as drug-addled behavior. For one thing they weren't doing that much. Not yet."[146]

By the end of that summer the Stones' inner sanctum was visited by experimental filmmaker Kenneth Anger, a devotee of the epochal occultist Aleister Crowley. The 40-year-old fanatic had **LUCIFER** tattooed across his chest and a wealth of esoterica to dish out for their impressionable young minds. Keith and Anita and Mick and Marianne "listened spellbound as Anger turned them on to Crowley's power and ideas."

[144] Wells, p. 116
[145] Ibid p. 113
[146] Faithfull, pp. 126-129

"I did have an interest in witchcraft," Anita acknowledged. "In the black magicians that my friend, Kenneth Anger, introduced me to. The world of the occult fascinated me."

"She was obsessed with black magic," recounted Tony Sanchez, her regular heroin dealer. "[Anita] began to carry a string of garlic with her everywhere- even to bed- to ward off vampires. She also had strange mysterious old shakers for holy water, which she used for some of her rituals. Her ceremonies became increasingly secret, and she warned me never to interrupt her when she was working on a spell."[147]

On one occasion Sanchez happened upon a trunk of hers which he assumed held her drug stash. He was horrified to discover it contained dead animal parts and wrinkled skin.[148]

Anita knew "all about witchcraft," according to Marianne Faithfull and Christopher Gibbs.[149] Her obsession with hocus-pocus led to a trip to Rio de Janeiro at the end of 1968, with Faithfull, Jagger and Richards.

"We have become very interested in magic and we are very serious about this trip," Richards told reporters beforehand. "We are hoping to see this magician who practices both white and black magic. He has a long and difficult name which we cannot pronounce- we just call him Banana for short."[150]

As they took the 10-day cruise to South America an older English couple on the ship repeatedly asked Jagger and Richards who they were. They refrained from identifying themselves but the woman kept needling "Just give us a glimmer"- meaning "Just give us a glimpse of who you are." Mick and Keith were so amused then and there they became the Glimmer Twins- a moniker which has stuck more than 50 years.

Faithfull had brought along her three-year-old son who didn't take to the Brazilian heat and they flew back to London, leaving the others to trek into Peru to search for UFOs. Whatever had transpired in Rio, she only

---

[147] Wells, pp. 189-190

[148] Anger: The Unauthorized Biography of Kenneth Anger by Bill Landis, Harper Collins (1995) p. 167

[149] Trynka, p. 160

[150] Jagger's black witch: She famously slept with Mick and had three children with Keith Richards. But a new book reveals Anita Pallenberg's love life wasn't half as crazy as her obsession with black magic, vampires and spells by Polly Dunbar, Daily Mail 2/22/20

elaborated, 25 years later, that "in Brazil the situation among Mick, Keith and Anita seemed to boil up into a lethal brew. I never understood quite what was going on. I felt I was there for some psychic, magical reason, but whatever the hell it was I never understood."[151]

At this point in their careers- while Brian was phasing out of the illicit drug use over at Cotchford- Mick and Keith (and their women) were in the beginnings of a serious heroin addiction. Unbelievably, in those days heroin could be acquired with a prescription at the local pharmacy; an addict simply had to register with the government to obtain high-grade and uncontaminated pills. And syringes.

According to Faithfull, "it was soon after *Performance* finished shooting in the fall of 1968 that drug use among our inner circle took a quantum leap."[152]

Performance was Jagger's inaugural and Pallenberg's third film. It was a chic look at decadence in the late 60s, "a psycho-sexual lab… a seething cauldron of diabolical ingredients: drugs, incestual sexual relationships, role reversals, art and life whipped together in a bitches' brew."[153] Again, according to Faithfull, "it was right after *Performance* that Anita really went off her rocker. For years. Into an abyss."[154]

Stash attempted to minimize the disreputable aura that Anita brought on herself with her black magic infatuation. "It's pretty ridiculous, this 'Anita and the occult' or 'Anita the Witch Queen' sort of thing," he opined years later. "I was one of the people who knew her well at the time and I can tell you, it's all rubbish. Keith hated all that stuff. This whole thing is just someone's Halloween dream."[155]

"She was never a staunch devotee," Faithfull concurred. "It's just that drugs inflate you to a point where you start to believe you really do have arcane powers."[156]

---

[151] Faithfull, p. 164

[152] Ibid p. 155

[153] Inside the sordid Mick Jagger film that horrified Hollywood by Rachel Laneri, NY Post, 1/25/20

[154] Faithfull, p. 155

[155] Wells, p. 191

[156] Faithfull, p. 187

In short, by the end of 1968 Anita was crackers. Heroin. Cocaine and hashish. Dead animal parts. Black magic spells. Garlic and holy water. A bright young mind brimming with esoteric mumbojumbo, a labyrinth of oracles without right angles.

Do you think Keith Richards was immune to her consultations? Might not some rather dark aspects of her persona have eroded his own questionable moral fiber?

That autumn the Stones had finished recording **Beggars Banquet**, an album that featured the hell-raising opening track *Sympathy for the Devil*- an epic ode to Lucifer punctuated in the background by 354 'woo-woo's. "An uplifting song," Richards later reflected. He had spiked in sharp jazzy riffs to enhance a Samba- rhythmed folk ballad. "It's just a matter of looking the Devil in the face. He's there all the time. I've had very close contact with Lucifer. I've met him several times."[157]

With the fate of Anita Pallenberg went the fate of the Rolling Stones. And after she abandoned Brian Jones in Morocco, he lost the will to battle Mick and Keith for supremacy in the band and he drifted further and further into a haze of drugs and alcohol. His romantic life devolved into a series of pseudo-doppelganger blondes like Nico, Suki Potier and Anna Wohlin.

"What I firmly believe to be the turning point in Brian's life was when he lost the only girl he ever loved," his father told the BBC in 1971. "I think this was a very severe blow to him. He changed quite suddenly, and alarmingly, from a bright, enthusuastic young man to a quiet, morose, and inward-looking young man- so much so that when his mother and I saw him for the first time for some months after this happened, we were quite shocked by the change in his appearance, and in our opinion, he was never the same boy again."

While unpacking his belongings during the move to Cotchford, Brain came across a photograph of himself and Anita. His father heard him whisper her name over and over again.

---

[157] Sympathy for the Devil- where Mick Jagger dabbled in the occult by Ian Gittins, Financial Times, 8/9/21

"Thank Christ, it was only Brian," she said to Tony Sanchez after his death.[158] **"Anita went through hell from survivor's guilt and guilt plain and simple**," Faithfull observed. "She developed grisly compulsions. One of them was that terrible business of cutting out pictures of Brian [from magazines] and sticking them up on the wall and then in the morning tearing them all down. It was a recapitulation of what Brian used to do with his tapes."[159]

In an interview a few years before her own death Pallenberg made a passing comment about Jones' death: "I'm sure if, uh- **that accident or whatever they call it**- wouldn't have happened to him- I'm sure he would have had another career. And he was- obviously he was upset- but he still- he still had the- as I say, he went to see Alexis Korner to reform a group, I mean. He was a trooper, you know. A musician."

It was apparent that she was confused on how to characterize the manner of death. And that she knew full well that the official story- drowning while under the influence of drugs and alcohol- was open to interpretation. And if one reads between the lines, one has to wonder whether she had direct knowledge of what actually happened.

Neither Anita nor Keith attended the funeral.

---

[158] Wells, p. 197
[159] Faithfull, p. 180

86

NINE

KENNETH ANGER

K enneth Anglemyer was a Hollywood kid who grew up to become a self-styled "magician-filmmaker".[160] He made his first film at age 17 and it would win a prize at the 1948 Festival of Damned Film held in Paris, winning the esteem of prominent avante-gardist Jean Cocteau. And it introduced his signature motifs of erotic surrealism, homosexuality and the occult- themes which laid a reputation in underground cinema that was rivaled only by Andy Warhol. And Anger also wrote, in 1958, the first of his photo-exposés on the dark underbelly of celebrities' personal lives, *Hollywood Babylon.*

As a boy Kenneth had immersed himself in the books of the 19th-century kabbalist Éliphas Lévi. He was thereby convinced, due to the resemblance of the microcosm to the macrocosm, that ritual magic could invoke the elemental forces of the cosmos both externally and internally, within the practitioner. The Devil is the inverse of God, and evil could thus be used as a means to achieve good.[161]

Soon he became a devotee of Aleister Crowley, the founding father of modern-day occultism. Crowley espoused a libertine philosophy of "Do what thou wilt," the basis for a magico-religious doctrine he created, known as Thelema. Its followers were encouraged to align their own will with the Cosmic Will which pervades the universe; this was furthered by practicing sex magic rituals, often under the influence of hard drugs like

---

[160] Landis, p. 8
[161] Ibid p. 26

87

cocaine and heroin. Crowley's prolific writings encompassed paganism, gnosticism, ceremonial magic, tarot cards and eastern mysticism. Anger was one of his lifelong admirers, and he stunned Jimmy Page- another Crowley obsessive- with his in-depth knowledge when they finally met in 1971.[162]

In addition to Cocteau, he also socialized with the erotic diarist Anaïs Nin, who starred in one of his films. He made a pilgrimage to the Thelema Abbey in Sicily- where Crowley had once maintained a religious commune- with sexual behaviorist Alfred Kinsey. And in the 60s he joined a discussion club run by Anton LaVey, founder of the Church of Satan.[163]

He had recently been a housemate of Marjorie Cameron, the widow of eclectic rocket scientist Jack Parsons. Parsons had been an ardent

Kenneth Anger in 1966

Thelemite occultist and was one of the formative figures in the creation of the Jet Propulsion Laboratory. According to actor Dennis Hopper, Marjorie Cameron was an "out and out witch... she and her husband had been involved in Aleister Crowley-type animal sacrifices in Pasadena and so on and had large groups of people involved."[164]

Birds of a feather flock together, and Anger was out on a limb all of his own two years before he met the Rolling Stones. He told reporters, "I know of the existence of a beautiful Mexican child who is being held captive by scientists in Los Angeles.

The child is now two years old. It is very intelligent. It has one beautiful perfect eye in the middle of its forehead and that is all. And the scientists- the doctors- they've got this child in an isolated clinic room and there are no mirrors and it has never seen another child. And the mother, of course,

---

[162] Ibid p. 183
[163] Landis, p. 155
[164] Ibid p. 72

when she heard she had some kind of freak, looked at it for maybe a split-second and screamed for the saints. They took the baby away and she's never seen it since. It's like the child has just been born out of a seashell.

The Cyclops child could lead the world."[165]

Marjorie Cameron's painting of her husband Jack Parsons as the Angel of Death

Whenever Anger was on the losing side in a dispute he would make threats in the form of Crowleyan curses.[166] Anywhere he lived he immediately painted a magick circle on the floor.[167] This is a pentagram inscribed within a circle, inside of which the magician renders words and gestures aimed at invoking- or otherwise banishing-assistance from the entities in the spirit world. The ceremony may be accentuated by the use of robes, candles, daggers, skulls and potent drugs.

Sigil of Baphomet

Robert Fraser

---

[165] Ibid p. 128
[166] Landis, p. 115
[167] Ibid p. 178

Once Kenneth Anger gravitated toward Swinging London in the summer of 1967, he immediately moved into art dealer Robert Fraser's Mount Street apartment. "Groovy Bob" had a gallery in the basement at Indica Books. He was a fellow homosexual with an appetite for drugs and his flat was a frequent haven for mind- altering parties. Attendees included the Rolling Stones. Fraser had also been busted in the Redlands raid that February, for the possession of heroin.

When they finally met, Anger had more than a few arrows in his quiver than simply mesmerizing the Stones with his Crowleyan prowess. He had a mutual friend with Pallenberg- the Uruguayan poet Gerard Malanga- who'd shared the house with Marjorie Cameron,[168] and kept in touch with Anita since her early modeling days.[169] And he had a deep understanding of the myriad ways that heroin, cocaine, amphetamines and hallucinogens can effect their "magick" upon various individuals.

Jagger was considering sidework in the movies and found Anger to be an engaging storyteller. He was very impressed with his reputation in avante-garde film. The frontman for the Stones saw occultism from a marketing perspective; it could help sell darkness and alienation to the cynical counterculture. He could personify it in his own performance art. Anger actually claimed that the song *Sympathy for the Devil* arose out of discussions he had with Jagger about Lucifer.[170]

"Kenneth was obsessed with the Stones," Marianne Faithfull insisted. He claimed to have seen a third nipple on Brian Jones' inner thigh,[171] and he "believed Mick, Keith, Anita and I all had one. He clearly had a crush on Mick and for a while Mick indulged him. He was entertaining and appropriately creepy, but when… he took to hurling copies of William Blake through the windows of [our apartment], Mick took all of our magic books and made a great pyre of them in the fireplace."[172]

But he did have them under his spell for a couple of years. Their narcissistic and gilded egos were perfect fodder for his Crowleyan machinations. Anger asserted that "the occult unit within the Stones was

---

[168] Ibid p. 101
[169] Wells, pp. 15-16
[170] Landis, pp. 163-164
[171] Trynka, p. 160
[172] Faithfull, p. 160

Keith and Anita and Brian. I believe that Anita is, for want of a better word, a witch."[173]

Marianne Faithfull in 1967

He proclaimed Richards as "his right-hand man". And he began making trips out to the Redlands estate, where Pallenberg would enthusiastically host him, in awe of his magickal mastery. Anger convinced her to carry garlic and protective tokens to ward off vampires.[174]

Early one morning Keith and Anita awoke to discover Anger pacing around a magick circle he'd made out on the huge estate lawn. He was wrapped in psychedelic scarves and doing funky dances under the moonlight.

Back at their London apartment, with a baby on the way, they began planning for marriage and opted to make it a true pagan wedding. It would include a hand- fasting ceremony and Kenneth Anger, as a grand magus, would preside. He explained to them that "the door of the house where the marriage ceremony is to be held must be painted with gold with a magical paint containing special herbs, which represent the sun."

After he left for the evening they fell into a deep narcotic slumber, and he returned shortly thereafter to paint the inside of the door in gold. Anita woke up astonished and exclaimed, "He can fly into the house any time he wants to!"

Keith, however, was pissed off that his expensive security system had been breached. "I don't want to go through with any black magic wedding," he suddenly decided. "This has gone far enough." Never realizing, of course, that he'd left his house unlocked.[175]

---

173 Landis, p. 166
174 Wells, p. 191
175 Landis, p. 167

Kenneth employed Mick Jagger to compose the soundtrack for his latest film, *Lucifer Rising*, a kaleidoscopic initiation into the terrors of the occult. He soon changed the title to **Invocation of my Demon Brother**. Jagger had a new Moog synthesizer and compiled the 11-minute improvisations in one night.

In December of 1968, for an intended BBC television special **Rock 'n Roll Circus**, Jagger unveiled a temporary tattoo of the face of Lucifer as he slowly writhed out of his shirt during a performance of *Sympathy for the Devil*. By this point he was tapping into the gestalt of using the occult as performance art. "**Keith and Anita later got into the black magic stuff**," Marianne Faithfull observed. "But Mick never got into magic any more than he got into drugs. He's a dabbler."[176]

On June 7, 1969, Richards was taking Pallenberg- seven months pregnant with their first child- home to Redlands in a rebuilt Mercedes that had once belonged to the Gestapo. He rounded a country bend at excess speed and lost control of the car and it flipped over three times

---

[176] Faithfull, p. 187

before coming to rest in a ditch. Anita broke her collarbone and had to be rushed to the local hospital. Richards hid all of his drugs and paraphernalia in an oak tree at the scene of the crash.

"When they returned to Redlands they got hold of everything Kenneth Anger had ever given them," Stash de Rola recalled. "Then they burnt

everything frantically so there was no possible hex on them. But it was just Keith falling asleep at the wheel; it had nothing to do with witchcraft."[177]

The next day Richards buddied up with Jagger and Charlie Watts and made a surprise visit to Cotchford Farm. They informed Brian Jones he was no longer a member of the Rolling Stones, the band he had founded. Although the split was ostensibly amicable, when they left Jones sat by the pool and sobbed uncontrollably for hours.[178]

On June 12th Pallenberg phoned Jones from London. She sounded distressed. But when he was asked what the call was about, Jones became abusive.[179]

---

[177] Wells, p. 196
[178] Wecht, p. 153
[179] Fitzgerald, p. 235

TEN

A GLIMMER OF JEALOUSY

"**N**ever, ever would I say that the atmosphere of the Stones was relaxed and happy. These five incredibly strong personalities were guarded, controlling their emotions. They weren't very open with *each other*, so they certainly couldn't have appeared to be relaxed to outsiders! There was rarely any outburst. It was just this tension, a moodiness, sulking... They took themselves a bit too seriously sometimes- yet I believe their tension helped the music."[180]

Astrid Lundström's observations pertained to the Stones camp since 1967, when she became Bill Wyman's girlfriend. The mild-mannered bassist didn't do drugs at all and kept a diary of his time with the band upon joining up in January of 1963.

Budding tensions within the band would grow into lingering animosity after an incident that September concerning "that stupid five quid."

Back in May of 1962 Brian had started the Rollin' Stones by putting an advertisement in *Jazz News*. Pianist Ian Stewart was the first to respond. The following month Mick and Keith enlisted from a Dartford hometown combo they'd been playing in, Little Boy Blue and the Blue Boys. And Charlie joined up just before Bill.

Jones chose the name from a Muddy Waters song, *Rollin' Stone Blues*. That name would officially be changed in 1963 to the Rolling Stones.[181]

---

[180] Stone Alone: The Story of a Rock 'n Roll Band by Bill Wyman, DaCapo Press (1990) p. 394
[181] Ibid p. 114

Mick had previously been singing with Alexis Korner's Blues Incorporated- Brian's former group- but wouldn't join the new band unless Keith was included. "Take one, don't take them both," Korner advised his pub circuit protégé, sensing that Jones would eventually lose control of his own band if he added both Dartford boys.[182]

Not only was there a hostile takeover as the Stones proceeded to evolve into a corporate juggernaut. Jagger and Richards essentially airbrushed Jones from the history of the band- badmouthing him for decades, downplaying his influence and sponge-jobbing episodes from their ascendant years. When a plaque was put up in 2020 at the Dartford train station, commemorating where Jagger and Richards reunited by chance in 1961 "and went on to form the Rolling Stones," Wyman was upset enough to threaten a lawsuit if that bit of fake history wasn't corrected.

"In 1963 Mick was simpy the singer," Wyman attested. "There was no doubt whatsoever who led the group in every way. Brian called the shots partly because he had pulled the musicians together, but mainly because what mattered most at that stage was music, and Brian was by far the most knowledgeable about what we were playing… The Stones took its musical stance entirely from Brian's passion for American rural blues music."[183]

---

[182] Trynka. P. 70
[183] Wyman, p. 114

Jones wrote doggedly to media outlets in search of auditions and gigs. He managed the finances. He chose the songs to play. He arranged the instrumentation. "Brian was so determined to be a star at any price," said club manager Giorgio Gomenski.[184] Journalist Peter Jones added, "He could tell you how much material they had and exactly where it came from. It was he who laid down the guiding policies of the band. It was Brian who supervised every single move that they made. He talked about Muddy Waters, Jimmy Reed and people like that. But he was in no way super-optimistic."[185]

With his mop of blond hair and musical virtuosity, Brian was a magnet for the girls who attended their performances. But the flamboyant lead singer Mick Jagger began to compete for his natural share of recognition from the audience and in the press; the allies on stage were destined to become bitter rivals away from the spotlight.

These eager and untamed rhythm & blues players caught the attention of Andrew Loog Oldham and Eric Easton, who signed Brian Jones (on behalf of the Rolling Stones) to a three-year management contract in May 1963. Oldham recalled, after their initial meeting after a gig at the Crawdaddy Club, "Brian put himself forward as the leader of the group and the rest seemed to accept this."[186]

---

184 Ibid p. 136
185 Ibid p. 129
186 Wyman, p. 132

Oldham was a 19-year-old street hustler who had done some minor publicity for a couple of Beatles hits. Easton was a middle-aged record producer who had recently launched his own company, Impact Sound. A subsequent recording contract gave Impact control of the Stones' master tapes. These were soon leased to Decca Records for a 14% royalty. But the Stones only received 6%, and an additional deduction for the management fee reverted them to 4.5% against Oldham/Easton's 9.5%.[187]

Oldham immediately dropped Stewart from the band's on-stage lineup; he was retained as tour manager and regular studio musician. Stu had had a bad case of childhood measles that left him with a lantern jaw. He didn't fit in with the street-gruff image that Oldham wanted to project. After he was cast aside, Stewart became increasingly bitter with Brian, who'd made him false promises as to how the royalties would be split up.[188] "Brian was Welsh, and Welsh people are very devious," he complained.[189]

In September 1963- after a television appearance in Birmingham on *Thank Your Lucky Stars*- Jones, Wyman and Watts drove back to London in Stewart's VW van, sandwiched between all their equipment. Jagger and Richards rode back in Oldham's car, and he promptly moved into their apartment on Mapesbury Road. Thus began what Ian Stewart would christen 'the Unholy Trinity'.[190]

A month later, up in Liverpool, Stewart discovered that Jones was being paid £5 more per week than the other members of the band. It was an arrangement he had made with Eric Easton, unbeknownst to the others.[191] They were furious, despite the fact that their average individual take at that time was £193 per week, and he was shouldering more responsibilities. This trivial perceived slight would fester into dangerous animosity for the remainder of Brian's years with the Rolling Stones. "Everybody freaked

[187] Allen Klein: The Man Who Bailed Out the Beatles, Made the Stones, and Transformed Rock 'n Roll by Fred Goodman, Houghton Mifflin Harcourt, New York (2015) pp. 86-90
[188] Wyman, p. 133
[189] Trynka, pp. 128-129
[190] Wyman, pp. 149-150
[191] Trynka, p. 112

out," Richards remembered. "That was the beginning of the decline of Brian. We said, 'Fuck you'."[192]

It was at Mapesbury Road that Oldham- as the legend goes- locked Jagger and Richards in the kitchen and refused to let them out until they'd composed a song. He understood there would be a limit to playing cover versions. Success would be had with fresh material like the Beatles. Oldham envisioned another Lennon/McCartney partnership, which was retooling pop music via their own songwriting, rather than relying on professionals. "Once he moved into the same house as Mick and Keith, it immediately became those three on one side, Brian, Charlie and me on the other," Wyman recalled.[193] Oldham had been spellbound by Jagger at the Crawdaddy and went all in on him for the band's future. "Pop music is sex, and you have to hit them in the face with it," he stated. "Andrew only had eyes for Mick, and his supreme talent was that he could manipulate Mick," his PR man Tony Calder said.[194]

It became obvious that Oldham was encouraging a whispering campaign against Brian Jones.[195] The Stones' van was known to drive off without him for the next gig. And his songwriting efforts were ridiculed. "There were definitely acetates of his stuff," Calder remembered. "I played one to Andrew and said, 'This is not a bad song!' Andrew's response was 'Fuck off!' And of course Mick wasn't interested in singing it. They were cruel. Cruel fuckers."[196]

During the recording of *Little Red Rooster*- which showcased Brian's slide guitar, and became (to everyone's surprise) their first #1 hit in Britain- he was tricked into playing without the rest of the band. Jones arrived at the studio to find a note left on a chair, instructing him to overdub at selected places.

[192] Wyman, p. 158
[193] Ibid p. 171
[194] Trynka, p. 152
[195] Wyman, p. 172
[196] Trynka, p. 138

He was continually manipulated and humiliated at the Stones' sessions.[197] Brian would be left guessing about Mick and Andrew, since they seldom showed their true colors around him. But "Keith would be at Brian all the time... often plain, bloody nasty," Dawn Molloy recalled.[198] She had been a fixture at the studio in 1964 and bore Jones' son the following spring. "If something was going on, he'd pick a fight.

They might be throwing things around- and he'd hammer it, then throw things at Brian so it really hurt. He was nasty. It was very unhealthy."[199]

As his hold on his brainchild began slipping away, so did his hold on reality. Brian turned increasingly to drink and drugs to numb his sense of despair. With his asthma and probable bipolar condition- coupled with his high intelligence and fragile self-esteem- Jones seemed to sense intuitively that the power struggle for the musical direction of the band could not be won. This fight wasn't worth the cost.

"Mick and Keith got away with murder because Bill and Charlie didn't create any waves," Lundström said. "[They] *enabled* Mick and Keith to carry on what I considered to be incredibly selfish... It was tension, tension

---

[197] Ibid p. 190
[198] Ibid p. 293
[199] Ibid pp. 131-132

all the time… [Jagger and Richards] thought of themselves as having some sort of power or right, and they'd basically decided to be in charge."[200]

By 1965 Oldham was spurring Richards to begin singing during the recording sessions, since he wanted the image of a duet with Jagger. And he also began turning off Jones' microphone or fading out his instrument in mixes.[201] "It's time we got rid of him," he confided to his housemates.[202]

A Scottish artist, Dave Thomson, grew close to Jones and was the first outsider to notice his isolation from the rest of the band. "Brian was paranoid because he had a reason to be," Thomson related. "It was a paranoia based on reality. In a hotel I saw Brian standing outside a room with his ear to the door. When he saw me he said, 'They're talking about me. Go in and find out what they're saying'. And when I went in, I found out he was right. Brian was definitely being excluded. He thought Mick was at the root of it."[203]

Jones told Nicholas Fitzgerald that Jagger's "ambition was insatiable. He wanted to be *the* Rolling Stone… he was ruthless and unscrupulous and wouldn't let anyone stand in his way [and] would get rid of anyone who tried to… He needed to dominate not only the other Stones but the entire international rock scene."[204]

A month after appointing New York mogul Allen Klein as his personal business manager, Oldham attended a party on his private yacht along the Hudson River. They went to see the Beatles play at Shea Stadium. Keith Richards was with them and the three of them openly discussed removing Brian Jones from the Rolling Stones.[205]

[200] Wyman, pp. 175-176, 404

[201] Ibid, pp. 177-178

[202] Trynka, p. 139

[203] Wyman, p. 263

[204] Fitzgerald, p. 106

[205] Trynka, p. 162

Yet Brian remained the center of attention- especially with the girls-despite the stage antics of Mick and Keith. Later in 1965 he won a reader's poll in the *Record Mirror*- ahead of Paul McCartney- for Most Handsome Pop Star. He had become the 3rd most-photographed person on the planet, behind Jackie Kennedy and Muhammed Ali. "Mick had this jealousy, that a lot of girls liked Brian," remembered insider Denny Bruce. "Brian just had a look, a way of moving around, that really excited the audience."[206] He radiated a charisma effortlessly- from his looks, and superlative musical talents.

Brian had the ability to get inside a song and layer in a tone color, or a counter- melody, that would make them magical. "He could pick up an instrument, whether it be an oboe or a mellotron, and he could change the aspect of the song so that it became a hit," Keith Altham stated. "He

---

[206] Trynka, p. 175

could make hit records." Stash de Rola agreed. "Brian was fundamental in making every one of those hit songs immortal by his contributions... everyone deferred to him in the studio... Brian was somebody that everybody looked up to."[207]

His romance with Pallenberg swung the power pendulum of the band back in his direction. And that fulcrum was anchored by his trend-setting fashion style, at the forefront of the 60s drugs-and-sex revolution. His fellow Stones followed his peacock lead. And contrary to later half-truths that nobody liked him, Brian was immensely popular with the fanbase, who were attracted to his subtle flair and vulnerability.

His down-to-earth sincerity- and far-reaching musicianship- won him lasting friendships with other pop stars, much to his bandmates' envy.

Jones' fan mail regularly matched Jagger and Richards' combined.[208] Yet Oldham continued to arrange interviews for the Glimmer Twins only. Mick and Keith were usually booked together in hotel rooms while they were touring, so they could keep writing songs. There seemed to be an unwritten rule that Brian would be kept down, and given no credit as a composer. "He was frightened to write anything because he would be laughed at," Thomson recalled.[209]

Many Stones songs were actually collaborative efforts. Mick and Keith would typically bring in a sketch of a song on guitar or piano, and then the whole band contributed to its completion. "It happened frequently that the basic ideas and middle bits by Brian, Charlie and me went into the melting pot during long studio sessions," Bill Wyman remembered. "But over a period of hours or days the origins of our suggestions disappeared."[210] And only Jagger and Richards received any songwriting royalties, through an arrangement that had been facilitated by Andrew Loog Oldham.

The Stones' accountant, Stan Blackbourne, beseeched Brian: "What on earth are you doing? You write some of these songs and you give the name over as if Mick Jagger had done it. Do you understand that you're giving 'em thousands of pounds?!... You're writing a blank cheque!"[211]

[207] Brian Jones: Life and Death of a Rolling Stone by Danny Garcia
[208] Rawlings, p. 157
[209] Wyman, pp. 355, 364, 369
[210] Ibid p. 383
[211] Trynka, p. 202

This was no more evident than on their highly-acclaimed 1966 album ***Aftermath***. Brian created the melody line for their smash hit *Paint It, Black* right in the studio,[212] and completed the sitar's whirling-dervish aspect at George Harrison's house. For *Lady Jane* he layered in an electric dulcimer that transported the tune back into the Baroque era. And he found a marimba in a corner of the RCA studio and five minutes later came up with a counter-melody for *Under My Thumb*, an exotic tempo that still percolates sixty years later.

"I would like to write but I lack confidence and need encouragement," he reflected. "If I take [something] into the studio they'll just mock it, won't use it." His efforts were met with flat-out personal disdain: "*You* can't write *songs!*"[213] On their American tour that year Brian dominated the sound of the band,[214] while graciously telling the press that Mick Jagger was "the best pop performer Britain's ever had" and he was proud of the progress the group had made.[215]

---

[212] Trynka, p. 187
[213] Wyman, pp. 177, 364
[214] Trynka, p. 195
[215] Wyman, p. 375

Yet during recording sessions, arranger Jack Nitsche was appalled by the rude treatment of Jones. "Mick and Keith can be really nasty," he confided to Denny Bruce. "Last night, Brian wasn't allowed to contribute to a song they were working on. He had a harp part he thought would work out. And they went, 'All right, go in the studio.' They made him do it five or six times, where he had blood on both sides of his mouth from wailing so hard on the harp. But they hadn't even rolled the tape."[216]

"Had he not gotten so heavily into drugs, I don't think he would have stayed so long with the Stones," Astrid Lundström stated. "He would have cracked."[217]

When Brian ran into Gene Clark of the Byrds he helped write their hit *Eight Miles High*. "I thought he should have got a credit, " Clark explained. "But he didn't care."[218]

Only Brian Jones could have taken a schoolboy's recorder and fashioned an Elizabethan melody that would become a #1 rock ballad- *Ruby Tuesday*. And he also contributed piano to the finished piece, yet again received no songwriting credit. "I was amazed... the way he played this thing," sound engineer Eddie Kramer recalled. "It was a descant, or the next step up, something you'd see in English schools. Mick and Keith- not to put them down- would never have thought of something like that."[219]

Bill Wyman found out- as would Mick Taylor in the 70s- that his ideas for songs would be tossed aside if they didn't gel in one or two takes, whereas the Jagger/Richards brand was given every opportunity to manifest itself. Wyman actually came up with the backbone riff for their smash hit *Jumpin' Jack Flash*. "Charlie and Brian began jamming with me and it sounded really good and tough," he recounted. "When Mick and Keith walked in they said, 'Keep playing that, and don't forget it- it

---

[216] Trynka, pp. 177-178
[217] Wyman, p. 404
[218] Trynka, p. 185
[219] Ibid p. 201

sounds great'."[220] And they received all the credit, and extra royalties, for its composition. Brian, from his Byrds' influence, added the jangly guitar flourish to the finished recording.

Oldham quit the Stones organization during the recording of the psychedelic *Their Satanic Majesties Request* album. He had an out-of-bounds cocaine addiction and was ignoring his responsibilities. Eric Easton had been let go two years earlier- soon after Allen Klein stepped in- and would successfully sue for breach of contract.

Eric had been Brian's management buddy and his departure augmented the bruised star's emotional tailspin. He attended the Cheltenham funeral.

Oldham did not attend. His juvenile mind games in the studio and mean-minded subtraction of Jones away from songwriting contributions were at the root of his demise. Andrew, Mick and Keith began to look upon Brian as little more than a sideman-[221] when the truth was, as Wyman has noted, that the founder was probably more talented musically than the rest

---

[220] Wyman, pp. 482-483
[221] Ibid p. 459

of the band combined. And they seized on his weakness and ripped him apart like a pack of wolves.

"With that triumvirate against him, he didn't have much of a chance," said disc jockey Scott Ross. "One time I was in a hotel in New York, me and Brian in one room, and in the next there was Mick and Keith- both of them getting at him, ganging up on him. I don't think he was overreacting [about his paranoia]. He was simpy outnumbered."[222]

They blamed him for the Redlands bust, because he had mouthed off shortly beforehand to a tabloid reporter (who mistook him for Mick Jagger) about his drug usage. "They had a vendetta, Mick and Keith, a real vendetta," Faithfull recalled.[223] They resented the fact that their wildly successful careers were the fruits of Brian's vision, guts and crazy-hard determination. And instead of lending a hand, they put their boots to his neck when he was down and needed their support. "[He] was another person with low self-esteem who needed to be helped. Not to be destroyed and humiliated and ground underfoot. Because that's what was going on."

Jones was also targeted by the British establishment, since his rebel image and dandified honesty posed a threat to the traditional gentrified mores. Stan Blackbourne characterized him as Public Enemy Number One. There were at least seven documented police attempts to make an arrest.[224]

"Yes, it is hash. We do smoke. But not the cocaine, man. That is not my scene," he pleaded with police during a surprise raid at Courtfield Road. "I am not a junkie. That is not mine at all."[225]

Stash de Rola, who was busted with him, believed the incident precipitated his decline much more than the loss of Anita Pallenberg. "An American guy latched onto Brian and introduced him to Mandrax, which are downers, and he became a pill-head and there was an utter transformation in his behavior. And Brian's decline began as a result of that court case… he took

[222] Trynka, p. 143
[223] Faithfull, pp. 98-99, 172
[224] Trynka, pp. 241, 267
[225] Wyman, p. 426

like a duck to water to these prescription pills, and started to overindulge in them. And then he became absolutely useless."[226]

"… He didn't consider himself a Stone anymore. I saw him in the studio, incapable of playing. I knew the end had come. Because normally Brian's musicianship in the studio was such that he would know if a note was a quarter-tone out of tune…"

"… Brian was haunted by the fear of going to jail. They dropped the charge against me and Brian was persuaded to plead guilty to a lesser charge- plea-bargaining. I said, 'Please, Brian, forget the plea bargain, plead Not Guilty, because you're not guilty.' But it was impossible to talk him out of pleading guilty."[227]

By the time of the ***Beggars Banquet*** sessions Jones was sinking deeper into his own pathos. "Physically he was starting to look dodgy," said film agent Mim Scala. "Blotchy. Pasty, and his hands were getting blotchy with swollen fingers. I'd done weekend acid but wasn't whacked out on a daily basis, like he was… Keith never stopped playing guitar, always had one in his hands. And Brian wasn't pulling his weight."[228]

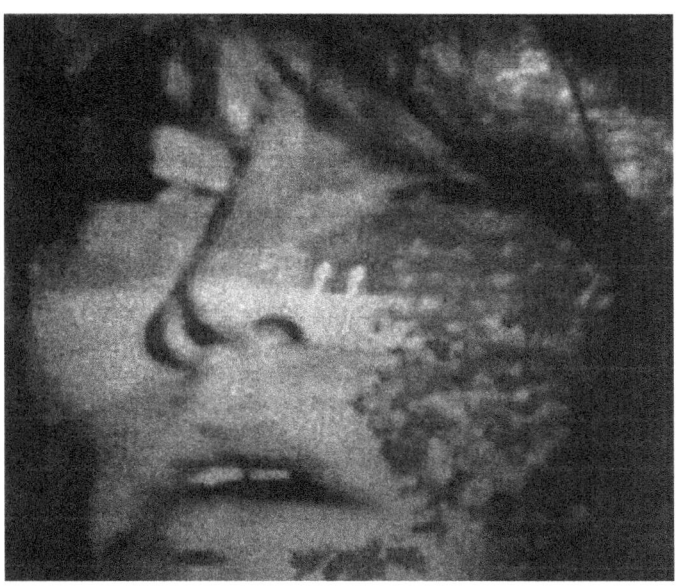

---

[226] Brian Jones: Life and Death of a Rolling Stone by Danny Garcia
[227] Wyman, p. 428
[228] Trynka, pp. 279-281

Yet despite Richards' later claims that Jones missed most of the sessions- and he had to fill in most of the guitar work- the logbooks show that Brian attended nearly every one. And the album credits list his multi-instrumental contributions on 8 of the 10 tracks.

In this time period, according to Jack Nitsche, Mick Jagger had transformed into an altogether different man. "[He] had this aloof look- where he looks down on everybody."[229]

Although keenly aware that he was being muscled out of his own band, Jones never once spoke disparagingly of his bully bandmates, staying loyal like an abused spouse. Instead, he took it out on his women. "Like an arsehole of the first order," Sam Cutler said. "He loved picking fights with his girlfriends."

Things went from bad to worse during the recording of *Let It Bleed*, where Jones only appeared on two tracks. "[Brian] couldn't play, he was physically incapable of holding a chord down," engineer Glyn Johns recounted. "It was pathetic. I didn't have a lot of sympathy for him, because he'd done it to himself."

Suki Potier recalled how Brian would get invited for a session, and "would turn up with [her] in the studio, sitting on a sofa waiting to be called in... then at five in the morning, it was 'See ya, Brian!' It was that way that he simply got railroaded out of the picture."

Marianne Faithfull found one of the letters he'd written to Jagger, asking him "please let me come back in... I'll play bongos, anything, but please let me come back in."[230]

Jack Nitsche told of a sinister episode that revealed a manipulative streak to Jagger's character. "Brian came up to me, looking pretty shaky, and asked what I thought he should do- he didn't know where he fit in. I told him to just pick up a guitar and start playing. Then he walked over to Mick and asked, 'What should I play?' Mick told him, 'You're a member of the band, Brian, play whatever you want.' So he played something, but Mick stopped him and said, 'No, Brian, not that- that's no good.' So Brian asked him again what to play and Mick told him again to play whatever he

---

[229] Trynka, p. 283
[230] Ibid, pp. 292-293

wanted. So Brian played something else, but Mick cut him off again- 'No, that's no good either, Brian'."[231]

Small wonder that during the course of a November all-nighter, recording takes of *You Can't Always Get What You Want*, Brian lay on the studio floor reading a biology textbook.[232] With his move to Cotchford his participation in recreational drug use tailed off, as did his participation in the Rolling Stones.

Peter Townshend performed in December's **Rock 'n Roll Circus** and was dismayed to see his old friend in such poor shape. "I took Mick and Keith aside and they were quite frank about it all; they said Brian had ceased to function, they were afraid he would slip away. They certainly were not hard-nosed about him. But they were determined not to let him drag them down- that was clear."[233]

By the end of February, on his 27th birthday, Jones had less than £4,000 in his bank account. He was hospitalized three days, for depression, in mid-March.[234] His last photoshoot with the band, on May 21st, was

---

[231] Ibid p. 302
[232] Wyman, p. 507
[233] Trynka, p. 299
[234] Wyman, p. 516

for the cover of ***Through the Past Darkly***, their second greatest-hits collection. The next day Jagger and Faithfull were arrested at their London apartment for possession of hashish and heroin.[235]

Richards, Jones and Jagger in London, September 25, 1968

On June 8th, at Cotchford, Jagger promised Jones a severance payment of £100,000 annually as long as the Rolling Stones made music.[236] But Mick didn't have that kind of liquidity at his disposal, because Allen Klein had a stranglehold on the Stones' finances. Klein was extremely upset when he learned about this informal business arrangement. He was quoted as saying that Brian would "never see a dime" of that money.[237]

Unbeknownst (apparently) to the other Stones, Brian had taken a trip to New York City late that spring. His guilty plea the previous year had prevented him from obtaining a *work* visa- a big reason for firing him from the band, since they were planning a long-awaited American tour at the end of 1969. But he was still eligible for a *travel* visa. Jones ran into clothier

[235] Rawlings, pp. 105-106
[236] Up and Down with the Rolling Stones by Tony Sanchez, Wm. Morrow, New York (1979) p. 138
[237] Voy Forums, 7/30/11

Gerry Seda in Greenwich Village and told her he was in Manhattan for "business AND pleasure". She had first met him with Bob Dylan back in 1968. In all likelihood Jones' business entailed a visit to Klein's offices in the Rockefeller Plaza.

Cheltenham punk rocker Jeremy Coleman had met Brian Jones as a child and spoke with Astrid Lundström about his death in 1984. She told him this was a completely taboo subject in the Stones organization. "There was something weird in her response," Coleman said. "It left me no doubt that people higher up the food chain knew about the circumstances of Brian's death."

Keith Richards, who claimed to *Rolling Stone* magazine in 1971 that he was using detectives to help keep the case open, was far more cynical in a *Q Magazine* interview in 1988. "I don't think you would find anyone who liked Brian. Brian was not a likeable guy. He had so many hang-ups, he was unreliable, he wanted to be a star. I admired his grit and determination… Listen, I'm being honest, right? I could say, oh yeah, Brian, lovely guy, but I'm being honest and he had so many hang-ups he didn't know where to hang himself so he drowned himself."

"I wasn't surprised when he died, not at all. There were extra hassles between Brian and me because I took his old lady. You know, he enjoyed beating chicks up, not a likeable guy. At the same time he had a likeable charm and we all tried to get on with him but he'd shit on you. It sounds like I'm putting him down but you ask anyone in the Stones and if they are honest they'll say the same thing."

"So no, I wasn't surprised about Brian. I didn't wish him dead and there were a few guys that did, but in all honesty it was no surprise, he was out there and I really don't think he expected to live."[238]

Forty-four years after the fact, during a world tour, the trio who had paid a visit to Cotchford to fire Jones were asked directly about his demise and death. "I always felt very sorry for Brian," Charlie Watts offered. "He was two things. He was not very nice, and he upset people very easily… We took his one thing away, which was being in a band."

"Do you remember what happened the day you went over there?" the interviewer asked.

[238] "Persona Non Grata," by Adrian Deevoy, Q Magazine, Oct. 1988

"No, I can't remember," Watts replied. "But I remember, it wasn't very nice."

"Fame doesn't sit comfortably on anyone's shoulders. Some people's shoulders it doesn't seem to fit at all," Mick Jagger laughed. "And he was one of them. You know, I don't think it suited him…"

"Keith and I took drugs. But Brian took too many drugs of the wrong kind and he wasn't functioning as a musician… I don't think he was that interested in contributing to the Rolling Stones anymore… You certainly didn't know if he was going to turn up and what state he was going to be in and then- what was he going to be able to do in that state? What job could you give him?"

Keith Richards added, "It was very important for us the fact that we're going to go back out on the road behind a new record that, uh- we resolved this thing with Brian…"

"And so Mick and I had to go down and so- tell Brian and virtually, like- 'Hey, you cock, you're fired'… You know, the fact that he was expecting it made it kind of easier, you know, he wasn't surprised. I didn't really think he took it all in. He was already up in the stratosphere, you know, it was kind of like, 'Hey, huh'…"

When asked how they learned of Brian's death, Richards recounted, "We were working in the studio with Jimmy Miller…"

And Jagger's voice is then spliced in: "… and someone came in and said, 'Brian's just died…'"

Richards continues: "Everybody just looks at each other and goes, 'Finally'… It was almost like it was bound to happen one way or another…"

"It was a horrible moment," Jagger went on. "And I don't know how many months later it was, when we went down to see him…"[239]

"It was three weeks," the interviewer reminded him, which was edited out of the film clip.

"Fuck," Jagger replied.

---

[239] The Rolling Stones: The Death of Brian Jones

There are four further sources for what actually transpired at Cotchford, which will be examined a bit later. They add disturbing details to a parting scenario that Charlie managed to admit "wasn't very nice".

Other than these brief interviews, there has been scant mention of Brian's contributions- or the terminal events at Cotchford- from surviving members (other than Bill Wyman) in the restless decades since. There was one tribute made- and only one- during their 2012 50th anniversary tour. The next year, revisiting the Hyde Park venue in London, his name wasn't even mentioned.

Their ongoing reticence begs the question: Is this silence born out of fear? Might not it bring a sorry end to their careers- and destruction of their legacy- if the truth about the Stones' involvment in Brian's death were brought to light?

Even further, is it also born out of guilt? Not in the sense that "we were young, we were selfish and immature… we were not understanding enough, we could have done more to help him out." But guilt stemming from direct connection to the murder of Brian Jones? [240]

One thing is deadly clear. Rock 'n roll is a cutthroat business. And Brian Jones, once the driving force in the band, by 1969 had become a major liability.

---

[240] Voy Forums, 7/24/11

ELEVEN

ALLEN KLEIN

As a young boy Allen Klein spent five years in Newark's Hebrew Orphanage, a place he often returned to show new clients like John Lennon. After enlisting in the Army and then studying accounting at Upsala College, he married Betty Rosenblum, almost ten years younger. She would one day become the B in his monolithic corporation ABKCO.

"Allen would have been a great psychiatrist and an even better trial lawyer," said its creative director Alan Steckler. "He could really *hear*; he was able to sort out people, their weaknesses and their needs. He could figure out what they needed and give it to them. That's why he was so successful with artists and with women. He was charming. And he was ruthless."[241]

In 1957 Klein joined a New York accounting firm, Joseph Fenton and Co., that specialized in music publishers. He didn't last because he liked to set his own work schedule and soon formed his own Allen Klein and Company for auditing the music business. "I learned a lesson," he reflected about his first accounting stint. "The artists never had any money. They were always paid with an advance, which they would spend, and then the sessions costs [also] came off their money. So they were always in the hole. And they were frequently represented by someone who didn't want someone else to come in and show them what they hadn't been doing right."[242]

---

[241] Goodman, p. 14
[242] Ibid p. 19

Conducting an audit on behalf of the rockabilly singer Buddy Knox brought Klein into contact with Morris Levy, president of Roulette records. Born Moishe, and nicknamed "The Octopus", Levy was widely regarded as the "toughest operator" in the music business, "someone you just don't fuck with."[243] His close childhood friend Vincent Gigante attempted to murder New York godfather Frank Costello in 1957; Gigante and several other Genovese crime family lieutenants often used Roulette's offices for card games, money laundering and heroin distribution.[244]

Morris Levy

Tommy James of the Shondells, who got finked out of $30 million in royalties, said that Levy once told him of stabbing the man who had killed his own brother and then "twisting the blade until his guts spilled out."[245] Levy conducted his end of the business with the help of blackmail and baseball bats. He habitually swindled artists out of song publishing royalties by fraudulently crediting the compositions to himself.

Klein would form a lifelong friendship with Levy and regularly visited his horse farm in upstate New York. The biggest gift at his son's

---

[243] Ibid p. 23

[244] Villains, Presidents, and Sixty Trucks Loaded with LA Cocaine: Organized Crime and the American Music Business by Michael Cronstrom, Kultur 3/19/19

[245] Sam Cooke: The Truth by B.G. Rhule, pp. 23-24

bar mitzvah- an Israeli bond- came from Morris Levy.[246] This criminal connection quite possibly was why Klein was denied his CPA license. Allen learned the tricks of the trade from Moishe and his gangster-negotiator career should be properly viewed through the lens of a lieutenant in a syndicate controlled by Vito Genovese and Sam Giancana. The mob, which initially infiltrated the business through jukeboxes and nightclubs, had a deadly chokehold on the lucrative music industry.

Before going on to conquer British acts such as the Dave Clark Five, the Animals, Herman's Hermits, Donovan, Lulu, the Kinks, the Stones and the Beatles, Klein landed big American talents Bobby Vinton and Sam Cooke. "The Polish Prince", Bobby Vinton, already had a manager at Epic Records but Klein promised him a million dollars, spead out over 20 years. "You sign with me and I'll get you out of your contract with your other manager."

"He was like a professor of life and deals," Vinton recalled. "He was just so bright compared to anybody else. And if he wasn't, he made you think he was. Yeah. He had the power of swaying everybody."[247]

Sam Cooke, "the Man Who Invented Soul", was suspicious that RCA was not giving him an honest accounting of record sales and royalties owed. This motivated him to establish his own record company, SAR- which would help find and record other artists- as well as his own music publishing company- Kags. Klein reminded him that RCA needed Cooke a lot more than Cooke needed RCA. He had the ability to write, perform and produce his own music. He needed them only for manufacturing, marketing and distribution.

Klein restructured Cooke's RCA deal and diverted some much-needed cash to the entrepeneurial singer. Sam was so pleased that he agreed to a five-year contract with Klein to administer to Kags Music and SAR Records.

He convinced Cooke to start his own record company for his own material, and this was named Tracey Ltd. in honor of his daughter. Tracey would produce and own all of Sam's recordings and manufacture the records. The exclusive distribution rights would then be sold to RCA. And to minimize Cooke's tax liability, Tracey would be set up as a holding

---

[246] Goodman, pp. 23-24
[247] Goodman, pp. 50-51

company that he would be paid for in preferred stock- taxable only when he converted dividends into cash.

It looked good on paper. But a year later Sam Cooke was found brutally murdered in a Los Angeles fleabag motel, clad only in a sportjacket and one shoe. He was shot through the heart while allegedly attempting to kidnap and rape a prostitute. Allen Klein was skeptical of the LAPD version of events and hired a private detective to investigate further.[248]

Klein repeated this procedure after the Brian Jones death, claiming he didn't trust the Sussex police. He discussed the findings of his detectives- the Klein Report- several times with Stones insider Sam Cutler. The overall conclusion was that Tom Keylock was directly responsible for Jones' death. But the Klein Report- whether or not it was ever eventually shared with police- has never surfaced.

Andrew Loog Oldham appointed Klein as his personal business manager a few days after meeting him in Miami in July 1965. He informed the press that "I manage the Stones, and Allen Klein manages the Stones and me." The band members, other than Bill Wyman, viewed him as a godsend. *Satisfaction* was topping the charts and they were beginning to realize how badly they'd been shafted- by both Decca Records and the Oldham/Easton slice of the royalties pie. Klein immediately marched them into Decca's London headquarters.

"I don't want you to say anything," he gristled. "Let me do the talking. You just sit there and look angry."

"I want to see royalty statements," he told Decca's chairman, Sir Edward Lewis. "You signed the band in 1963. It's 1965 and they've never received a royalty statement. I'd also like to see the license agreements for every territory. It's Monday. I'll be back tomorrow at the end of the day."

By Friday Klein had re-negotiated a one-year contract with a $600,000 advance against future royalties. He also severed the contract with Decca's American subsidiary, London Records- meaning they'd have to negotiate their own separate contract agreement if they wanted to sell Stones records in the U.S.A.

The band members each received dreamy fat checks and were ecstatic. A year hence and they would be richer than the Beatles. "Andrew sold him

---

[248] Ibid p. 57

to us as a gangster figure, someone outside the establishment," Mick Jagger related. "We found that rather attractive."[249]

Pete Bennett
Worlds Top Entertainment Promotion Man

Eric Easton was promptly let go and successfully sued Klein for breach of contracts that he, Oldham and Jones had signed in 1963. His lawyer Maurice Finer characterized Klein as "quite simply a predator in the field of pop artists." Easton was more blunt: "He eats people."[250]

Jones, Bennett, Wyman, Richards, Jagger and Watts

Jones actually recommended that Klein take over as the Stones' authorized manager, but his python grip was still a couple of years away. "I did not get one penny from the Stones," Klein maintained. "My money came out of Easton and Oldham's end."

With an American tour planned by the end of 1965, Klein convinced the band to let the William Morris Agency handle their bookings. He also set up a satellite company, Gideon Music- which Allen himself financed and administered- that would own the copyrights to their new and extant compositions. Not only did he guarantee 72 cents on every dollar- well

[249] Record Executive Allen Klein, 77, dies by T. Rees Shapiro, Washington Post, 7/08/09

[250] Wyman, pp. 466, 472

above the standard 50/50 split- but he tacked on a million dollar advance, to be paid out in 20 annual installments.[251]

Allen's personal music promoter, Pete Bennett, began traveling with the band, and they quickly coined him "our Mafia promo man". Pete's major function was to ensure that disc jockeys coast-to-coast played Rolling Stones records. Four thousand of the 6,000 radio stations had playlists controlled by organized crime.[252] Born Pietro Benedetto, he had been working with Klein since 1963 and had helped Nat King Cole and Sam Cooke surge back into the Top 10.

Klein also created Nanker Phelge Music, a tax shelter for housing the rights to the master recordings, thereby controlling the ability to manufacture Rolling Stones records. They could then be leased to, for example, London Records, and thus enable the band to avoid the exorbitant British taxes on foreign income. Allen, of course, set himself up as the owner.

In the meantime, as their popularity grew and grew, Allen Klein deposited millions of dollars contractually owed the Stones into New York's Chemical Bank. And he used it for his own personal investment purposes.[253] In May 1966 he bought up a chunk of MGM Records for £ 1 million.

Strangely enough, the group's primary bank account at the time was over £4,000 in the red.[254] They had toured relentlessly, played to packed stadiums, had a dozen international hits- yet they were strapped for cash. Major purchases such as for a home were accomodated on a piecemeal basis, since Klein controlled the purse strings from New York. "If there is too much money readily available," he explained, "I feel it will only be squandered."

As 1967 started, the band members- excepting Wyman- still had a great faith in Klein as their financial savior. But they were paid only erratically, and he kept switching money around whenever they requested it. By year's end they had topped $100 million in sales, and had

---

[251] Goodman, pp. 105, 109, 137
[252] Cronstrom, Kultur, 3/19/19
[253] Goodman, pp. 122, 129
[254] Wyman, pp. 374, 376

approximately £ 3 million in the group account, before taxes.[255] Oldham
had just quit and handed the managerial reins over to Klein, who seems

to have been managing them all along,
and at a dizzying clip.

"Allen comes in when your harvest
is not as plentiful as your expectations
on the sow," Andrew later reflected.
"And part of the price is that he gets the
farm."[256]

That farm became Klein's the
following year as he bought out Oldham's
entire interest in the Stones, giving him
50% of all royalties for their catalogue
all the way back from 1963 on into
1971. This kindled roughly 17 lawsuits,
most of them ruled in Klein's favor.
Oldham claimed he didn't believe the
band members would be willing to pay
for their recording rights; Klein had the money and the desire. And he
reckoned a deal with Allen would help preserve some of his own leverage in
the music business. They never informed the band of Klein's intentions.[257]

The *Sunday Times* tagged him as "The Toughest Wheeler-Dealer in
the Pop Jungle" whom fortune favored because he could "lie like a trooper."
This was a cut below the waist, because Allen in fact worked doggedly
behind the scenes to create his own opportunities. He memorized every
piece of information he could find about his new prospects- press clippings,
contracts, associates, habits- and invariably lined himself up with the right
people at the right time to work out a deal. He was smart as a whip, always
well-prepared, determined and absolutely unscrupulous when it came to
making money, and more of it.

Klein delighted in his foul-mouthed reputation and take-no-prisoners
approach to music negotiations. "Don't talk to me about ethics," he

[255] Ibid pp. 385, 399, 476
[256] Goodman, p. 59
[257] Goodman, pp. 198-199

pontificated to *Playboy* magazine in 1971. "It's like a war. You choose your side early and from then on you're being shot at. The man you beat is likely to call you unethical. So what?" This kind of attitude brought him genuine affection for Keith Richards, alone among the Stones.[258] Keith had been the one who overruled Bill Wyman's initial distrust in 1965: "Don't be so fucking mercenary! We've got to trust someone!"[259]

But Wyman's fears were not illusory. In 1968 Klein created his signature enterprise, ABKCO Music & Records, Inc.- an umbrella corporation which encompassed management, music publishing and film & television & theatrical production. He ran it like a Jewish family business.[260] It handled all of the Stones' financing, advertising & promotion, manufacturing of records and getting them airplay. And, oh, Allen Klein wasn't simply their business manager. Because the phrase "in perpetuity" had wormed its way into the Nanker Phelge contracts, Klein was also their partner *forever*.[261]

In April the Stones finally hired an independent team of solicitors to look into their financial affairs.[262] But it wasn't until the following year that they began the process of formally breaking away from Klein, after Mick Jagger approached a London merchant bank manager with some clout, Prince Rupert Loewenstein.

Klein, in the meantime, had bigger fish to fry and began diverting his attention to courting the Beatles. He won them essentially by praising the disrespected Yoko Ono and lavishing John Lennon with the lyrics of hundreds of pop songs. John swung George and Ringo over to his side and by February 1969 Allen was the Fab Four's certified manager. Paul was never happy with the arrangement and called him "nothing more than a trained New York crook."

[258] Ibid, p. xiv

[259] Wyman, p. 329

[260] Goodman, p. 26

[261] Ibid pp. 144, 202-203

[262] Wyman, p. 485

Klein kept tabs on his clientele and rented a suite at the luxurious Dorchester Hotel, overlooking Hyde Park, whenever he was in London. This fastidiousness helps illuminate a critical phrase in the Sussex police statement of Tom Keylock, given the morning after Brian Jones' murder. Keylock stated that "I continued to look after his interests **under the order of Rolling Stones Ltd.**" This means he was ordered by his paymaster, Allen Klein, to keep him informed of Jones' personal affairs.

STATEMENT OF WITNESS

NAME: Thomas Richard KEYLOCK

OCCUPATION: Tour Manager

ADDRESS: 15 Outram Road, Alexandra Park, London, N.22

TELEPHONE NO: 888 - 3436

I am the Tour Manager for the Rolling Stones and until four weeks ago Brian JONES was a member of that group, but, I continued to look after his interests under the order of Rolling Stones Ltd. He was making tentative arrangements to form a new group.

I have known Brian for four and a half years. He has always been of a restless and nervous disposition. I have been in frequent contact with him up to the time of his death and last spoke to him by telephone at midday on Wednesday 2nd July, 1969 when he was his normal self and discussed with me his plans for a holiday and the formation of his new group.

Klein was in London at the time and apparently ordered the hit. And Brian knew it was coming. He had told Graham Bond in a London hotel room on the morning of the day before that "They are going to kill me!" He returned to the city the next day to visit the Stones office and "went back to Cotchford during the afternoon in a chauffeur-driven car hired by our office."[263] And on his final evening he pleaded with carpet-fitter David Gibson to stay over, because he was terrified for his life.

Keylock wasn't with Rolling Stones Ltd. for musical reasons and he knew where the money came from. He apparently carried out Klein's sinister orders, which included burning Brian's personal papers.[264] The coverup, as he stressed at the end of his life, "went right to the very top." This was a political murder that entailed control of Scotland Yard itself.

---

[263] Rolling With the Stones by Bill Wyman, DK ADULT, London (2002) p. 327
[264] Voy Forums, 7/24/11

No one but the Crown, the Home Office, or the international banksters had that kind of power.

It is an altogether surreal coincidence that Keylock's death- 40 years to the day after Brian's- was followed two days later by the death of Allen Klein. We can place good confidence in the conclusion that Klein was the warlord behind this long- concealed murder. This was not the first time he had snuffed out the life of a popular musical genius.

TWELVE

THE MURDER OF SAM COOKE

S am Cooke was a phenom, an entertainer on the order of Nat King Cole and Harry Belafonte, to whom he was often compared. He was a prolific songwriter who, beginning in 1957, charted more than thirty Top 40 singles such as *You Send Me*, *Cupid*, *Chain Gang* and *Another Saturday Night*. In 2008 *Rolling Stone* selected him as #4 among the greatest singers of all time.

He began as a gospel singer in a high school group with Lou Rawls, known as the Teenage Kings of Harmony.[265] Sam later joined the Highway Q.C.'s and then the Soul Stirrers before embarking on a solo career. His drop-dead good looks and natural ability soon won him a contract with RCA; his influence on contemporary music- crossing his gospel roots over into the pop culture- earned him the sobriquet "The King of Soul".

On a personal level, he was married twice. His second wife, Barbara, had been his junior high school sweetheart. She bore him three children: Linda, Tracey, and baby Vincent, who drowned in the family pool in July 1963. Women found him irresistible and he also fathered at least four illegitimate children.

In 1961 Sam joined forces with his mentor, J.W. Alexander, and his manager, Roy Crain, to establish SAR Records. Not only did this enable him to sell back his own music to RCA, and thereby keep an accurate accounting of copies pressed- which minimized the rampant under-the-table sales of promo copies. He also encouraged other R & B and

---

[265] Rhule, p. 33

gospel artists to sign on with SAR. They soon created Derby Records to focus on pop. Alexander had founded Kags Music a couple of years previously as a music publishing and management firm. Cooke began assigning songwriting credits to his wife in an effort to sidestep publishing agreements made earlier in his career.

Allen Klein stepped into his life in 1963, promising he could get back royalties due him from RCA. He could also return Cooke to the prestigious Copacabana, where he'd had difficulties four years previous. When Klein delivered on his tough talk, Sam was so impressed he signed him to a 5-year contract to administer to SAR and Kags. Little did he expect that, right from the beginning, Klein would start manipulating his secretary in his Los Angeles office.

"Get the copyrights out of the drawer!" he demanded of Zelda Sands, who also served as Cooke's labels manager for SAR and Derby. "I want to take them to New York!"[266]

---

[266] Rhule, p. 143

Klein was completely bankrupted in early 1964, due to a bad investment favored by his in-laws. To help promote the Copacabana engagement, in June he rented a huge billboard proclaiming his client "The Biggest Cooke in Town". What Sam didn't realize was that this advertising- as well as a gift of a Rolls Royce- was billed to SAR Records.[267]

By the end of the summer he convinced Cooke to set up his own company for his own material. Tracey Ltd. would own all the rights to Sam's music- his songs and produced recordings. These could then be leased for distribution in a separate agreement with RCA. Not only would his stock payments not be taxed until converted to cash; if they filed for incorporation in Nevada, that state didn't even tax entertainment. This could also lead to easier bookings at the Las Vegas casinos.

The original paperwork for Tracey Ltd.- filed by Allen Klein in September 1963- listed Sam Cooke as President, James W. Alexander as Vice President, and Allen Klein as Secretary. The Board of Directors listed Sam Cooke, James W. Alexander, S.R. Crain (Sam's manager) and Rev. Charles S. Cook (Sam's father).

What is missing from this document is a statement to shareholders. Instead, it contains a statement to the board of directors- who legally serve under the pleasure of the shareholders.

Under U.S. law, the shareholders are not required to be disclosed. According to the analysis of paralegal Donald Piper, Tracey Ltd. did actually have one unspecified shareholder, who had the power to change

---

[267] Rhule, pp. 114, 133

the board of directors, or to name a different person as president. That one shareholder was Allen Klein.[268]

On May 5th, 1964, in papers filed with the Nevada Secretary of State, Tracey Ltd. still listed Allen Klein as Secretary. Sam Cooke, however, was now listed as Chairman of the Board, under a subsection designating an "Officer who is not a Director". This document was signed only by Allen Klein. It certified that Cooke was now his employee. And colluding with Klein to get these papers authorized was Sam's partner since his gospel days, J.W. Alexander.[269]

Six months after Cooke's death, on June 17th, 1965, Tracey Ltd. proceeded to list Allen Klein as its President, James W. Alexander as Vice President, Henry Newfield (a business associate of Klein's) as Vice President, and Betty Klein as Secretary.

The final nail in the coffin came on March 31, 1970, when Tracey Ltd.- along with numerous other Klein satellites- was merged into ABKCO, Inc. The Sam Cooke catalogue, which stretches back to 1957, is worth approximately $100 million today.

And there is further suspicion surrounding the original articles of incorporation. It was signed in New York on September 27th, 1963, by Cooke, Alexander and Crain- and duly notarized. Yet on the night of September 26th Sam Cooke was performing at the Municipal Auditorium in New Orleans- and Alexander, Crain, and even Allen Klein were all down there with him. The New York notary also happened to be Klein's longtime secretary, Adrienne Theresa Zanghi. It appears that this document was undated when it was actually signed; the date was then filled in by the notary.

A few days before his death Sam Cooke had decided to go to New York and call a press conference to expose Allen Klein. Not only had he discovered that he and his father were no longer on the board of directors at Tracey Ltd. and that his titles were no longer in his name. For some strange reason money from SAR Records was going to a subsidiary, WL Records. He was planning on severing ties with Klein, who belonged in prison for extortion and fraud.

---

[268] The Killing of Sam Cooke: Who Murdered Soul? @ youtube.com
[269] Rhule, p. 99

The official police version of Sam Cooke's murder was that he had attempted to kidnap and rape Elisa Boyer at the Motel Hacienda in south

Los Angeles. She had gotten away from him and run off with his clothes. Wearing only a suitjacket, and leaving his new Ferrari running in the parking lot, Cooke broke open the office door looking for Boyer. The motel manager, Bertha Franklin, shot him in the ensuing scuffle. The bullet, although it entered under his armpit, went straight through his heart. The police ruled it a "justifiable homicide".

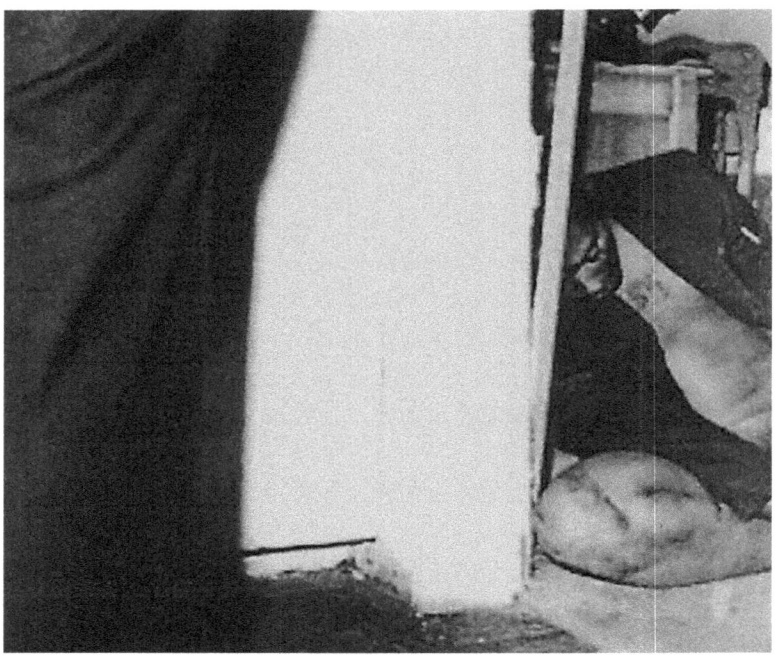

Fire captain Harry Woods arrived at the scene shortly after police. He noted that Cooke had suffered a "going over [with] a baseball bat." Both of his legs looked broken. The police story was "very fishy"; it didn't seem that these two women were capable of that kind of damage.

"They didn't have to kill him," his wife Barbara wept, sounding as though she knew he was going to get roughed up.[270]

Relatives who snuck into the mortuary said that "Sam was beaten head to toe. There were bruises all over his body, his knuckles and fingers were broken, knee caps busted, his shoulders looked dislocated... This was a deliberate beating meant to send a message, and a shooting to finish him off. We took photographs and attempted to persuade the LAPD that they had made a mistake in closing the case, but they had no interest whatsoever in hearing the truth. They simply wanted to keep it closed, even though they knew it was bullshit."[271]

---

[270] Rhule, pp. 167, 180, 204
[271] Ibid p. 159

Singer Etta James, seeing his mangled fingers within the glass-encased casket, remarked that his hands had been scraped profusely, like they were dragged across concrete.[272]

At the coroner's inquest both Elisa Boyer and Bertha Franklin wore sunglasses, to help hide their lying eyes. There was no chalk diagram of where the body was found. There were no photos of Cooke's clothing, allegedly discovered under a stairwell half a block away. But there plenty of photos of motel office paraphernalia and a damaged doorway that had no causal connection to the deceased. Elisa Boyer was not asked her real name- Crystal Chen Yung- and the judge would not allow questioning as to her occupation. He would have learned she was a prostitute and the Hacienda was a LAPD-connected whorehouse.[273]

Elisa Boyer   *Bertha Franklin*

Bertha Franklin claimed that when she struggled free from Cooke, she ran for her TV and grabbed her pistol off the console and fired three shots at him. Allegedly he cried out, "Lady, you shot me!" and ran at her again. As they kept fighting she hit him repeatedly with a stick until he collapsed on the floor.

All this, after sustaining a .22 bullet wound that- according to the testimony of the autopsist- "penetrated the left main pulmonary artery and vein, emerging through the posterior wall of the left atrium- that is, the

---

[272] Rhule, p. 194
[273] Ibid p. 167

left chamber of the heart- to enter the right lung." Sam Cooke must have died on the spot and never said a word. Zelda Sands recalled that "Allen's thugs escorted Boyer out of the courthouse."[274]

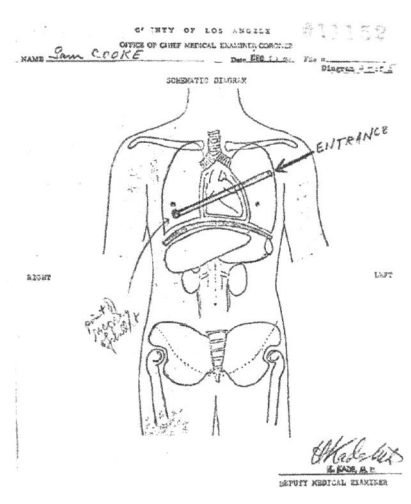

The Sam Cooke murder continued to be regarded with suspicion and the following inside information surfaced many years later, as related to blues guitarist Leo Eiffert. It was told to him by Angelo Spezze, a singer/songwriter who performed under the stage name Johnny Angel:

"He knew some of Klein's goombas. When Sam died, he told me he knew immediately Klein had something to do with it. I mean, he had absolutely no doubt whatsoever. So he and [his nephew] Kenny paid a visit to his goomba friends, very innocent-like, and somehow weaved in the subject of Sam Cooke. They not only told Johnny that Klein had ordered it because Sam was trying to dump him, but that it wasn't the inner circle that did the deed- it was several big-ass LAPD cops he hired and paid for with Sam's money. He told me, 'I knew it! I knew that bastard Klein had ordered it. You see, Leo, they take your weakness and exploit it. In Sam's case, it was women, because women found him irresistible and were always surrounding him. It was easy for people to believe Sam was a womanizer, even though that was not necessarily what was going down at the time. This bastard knew he could get people to believe Sam was a bad dude because 1) he was black, she wasn't, and it was 1964, and 2) he was black, she wasn't, and it was 1964."

"So then he told me exactly how it went down... The woman was a prostitute. She had worked for the LAPD before, so they used her as bait to get Sam to a cheap, seedy hotel in the worst part of L.A. where they could pay off witnesses and get the management to do whatever they wanted done... she delivered him to a room at the Hacienda Hotel, on

---

[274] Rhule, pp. 157, 235

Figueroa Boulevard. As soon as he opened the door, these thugs and off-duty cops were waiting for him, and gave Sam a pretty bad going- over.

Somehow, he slipped out and ran for his car. These dudes had a limo, OK? They jumped in and headed in Sam's direction, catching up with him as he was starting his car. They clubbed him, punched him, and quickly dragged him into the limo, where, in the darkness of night, and with a silencer, they executed him."

"They went through his pockets, got a huge roll of cash, maybe 10K, which was a lot of green back then, OK?...

They pull up to the front door of the motel, see the manager sitting there alone. Before busting down the door, they take all of Sam's clothes off- blood stains from the beatings would contradict their story- putting only his jacket on, which he had not been wearing. They arranged Sam's body against a wall, wave the cash at the woman and the hooker, telling them what their stories were going to be. They had no choice in the matter, anyway, OK? This was how it was going down, and if the manager had protested, they'd have shot her too, because they could have said that her gun went off in the struggle and Sam had accidentally shot her."

"So they arrange the office to look like a struggle had occurred, smear blood from Sam's body on her dress, instruct her to call the [motel's] owner to tell her that Sam busted her door down looking for a girl who ran off with his pants in the middle of his attempt to rape her, as they fire a shot for her to hear, and as the girl is dutifully calling LAPD to report that she was a kidnap and intended rape victim."[275]

---

[275] Rhule, pp. 154-156

Earlier that evening Sam had been seen "alone at the bar" at Martoni's Restaurant. He had an unreported two-hour conversation there with Gold Star Studios producer Stan Ross, who had engineered a **Shindig** television appearance of Sam's just that past September. "There was no girl anywhere near Sam," Ross maintained. "He nursed that drink for quite some time."[276]

After Ross went home, about 12:30 AM, what apparently happened is that Elisa Boyer aka Crystal Chen Yung was brought to Martoni's to meet Sam. She was brought there by Pete Bennett[277] the Stones' "Mafia promo man". Shortly thereafter Sam received a frantic telephone call from a good friend, SAR recording artist Johnny Morisette, begging him to hurry over to PJ's Nightclub on Santa Monica Boulevard.

Morisette's son- and Zelda Sands- each were later informed that Johnny Morisette in fact had a gun pointed at his head when he made this telephone call- and it was held by Allen Klein. Johnny's son stated that Klein "detested Sam [and] was jealous of his success." PJ's was a favorite hangout of mob boss Mickey Cohen and was managed by organized crime. It was also the last place Bobby Fuller was seen alive in 1966. The 23-year-old singer of the smash hit *I Fought the Law* was found soaked in gasoline in his car parked outside of his Hollywood apartment.

While at PJ's- according to Walter Wood of the doo-wop group The Olympics- Cooke was given a $10,000 advance by the owner after promising to perform there. Wood warned his friend that the girl he was with worked for the LAPD. But Sam ignored him and gave her a ride "home" to the Motel Hacienda.[278]

"I know you think I murdered Sam Cooke," Klein told Sands shortly after the funeral.[279] What is virtually certain is that Klein was at least in the limo when Cooke was executed- if not the actual triggerman. As he was savagely beaten and dragged from his Ferrari, Cooke was tossed into the back of a limousine that belonged to Allen Klein! "Klein didn't go anywhere without that stretch limo- his armed thugs inside," swore drummer Hal Blaine.[280]

---

[276] Ibid p. 161

[277] Ibid p. 102

[278] Ibid pp. 158, 163-164, 185-186

[279] The Killing of Sam Cooke: Who Murdered Soul? @ youtube.com

[280] Rhule, p. 158

Once he bled out, Cooke's clothing was stripped and he was tossed into the motel clad only in a fresh suitjacket and one shoe- a mob message to the L.A. police that this was our business: stay out of it.[281]

Hugo & Luigi with Sam Cooke   *J.W. Alexander*

Shortly after Sam's death his widow Barbara sold her share in the copyrights to Hugo Peretti & Luigi Creatore, a singer/songwriting team for Morris Levy's Roulette Records. "There never was any romance between them that Lou and I ever witnessed," Lana Rawls recalled. "She was as much an opportunist as the people in Sam's office who talked money 24/7. Barbara used Sam for the status of being Mrs. Sam Cooke and for the material things she never had. But we all knew she had a boyfriend up the street from the Hacienda."[282]

Hugo & Luigi would soon be paid off by Klein, as would J.W. Alexander, who was removed altogether from Tracey Ltd. And with the Sam Cooke catalogue all his own, Allen Klein now had the leverage to go after the British Invasion groups of the mid-60s. This would eventually bring him the treasure of Solomon's Temple.

Bennett became promotional manager for the Beatles following the suspicious death of their business manager Brian Epstein. Klein of course eventually succeeded Epstein and increased his corporate fortune at ABKCO, where Bennett worked as his promo man. The only minor consequences they ever faced were for income tax evasion for 1970-1972. Bennett escaped prison time by testifying against Klein, who served a paltry two months for making a false statement on his 1972 return.

---

[281] Ibid p. 182
[282] Ibid pp. 179, 202

The similarities between the homicides of Sam Cooke and Brian Jones are horrifyingly apparent. Allen Klein was the master of their financial affairs and ingratiated himself with key people in their inner circle. He knew the local police would only conduct a perfunctory investigation; meanwhile, his own detectives would ensure that no incriminating information ever surfaced against him. Any witnesses could be paid off, threatened into silence or ridiculed.

The coroner was likewise bought off. In Jones' case there was no mention of algae found in the lungs, and a false insinuation that drug residue found in the urine had contributed to an accidental drowning. In Cooke's case there was no mention of his obvious broken fingers and kneecaps, or the extensive bruises all over his body.[283]

And the finale was the control of the all-important press coverage. Sam Cooke could be sold to them as a reckless womanizer, his fatal flaw which did him in. Brian Jones could be portrayed as a hopeless drug addict who took it to the edge one too many times.

This type of character assassination not only helped to tarnish their legacies. It shifted the blame for their deaths onto themselves, and helped Allen Klein get away with murder.

---

[283] Rhule, pp. 194-195, 234-236

THIRTEEN

STEWED AND KEEFED

Early on the evening of June 8th Mick Jagger, Keith Richards and Charlie Watts paid a surprise visit to Brian Jones at his Cotchford estate to tell him he was no longer in the band. "The thirty-minute conversation was friendly and all parties were relieved that matters were reaching a conclusion," according to Bill Wyman. "Mick and Keith told Brian that the group could not go on working with him the way he was."

"There was a violent disagreement over the music."[284] This must have been what Charlie was alluding to in 2013, when he admitted that it "wasn't very nice".

Anna Wohlin was upstairs with Brian when they arrived. She said she went to the window and saw Mick's white Mercedes out in the courtyard. "I saw Mick, Keith and Charlie, but not Bill. They all had stepped out of the car and were on their way to the front door." And she decided it best to stay upstairs.

"… I could hear Brian showing them into the dining room and I wondered why Bill wasn't with them. Maybe he thought it would be ugly. He was right. I couldn't make out the voices, but there was plenty of talk and indiscriminate shouting. Strangely enough, it was Brian who seemed the more controlled. He'd prepared for this moment for a long time, even though he'd never thought the final decision would come so quickly."

Brian told her that they agreed to remain friends, and that he would get a financial settlement. He was also given a packet of cocaine from

---

[284] Wyman, p. 522

Keith, which he used up and it made him throw up several times over the course of the night."[285] [Note: This was probably heroin.][286]

In 1995 a young man studying at the Paris Sorbonne met an older woman there who confided she'd once been a girlfriend of Brian Jones, before he became so very famous. Her name was ZouZou and she regaled how she often heard Mick and Keith making cruel jokes about Brian at parties. He became more and more estranged within his own band and found an escape through drugs.

ZouZou "had been told by Brian that during the rather heated conversation concerning Brian being kicked out of his own band, that he had said it was ridiculous and that it was *his band and his name*- that in fact he had decided to start a new line-up anyway and that *they* were actually fired and not him!! And he started to laugh as he saw their faces turn pale when they realized that he was the band's creator officially and legally speaking."

"So then Keith pulled a knife on him. It was Mick that had stepped in to stop Keith from doing something stupid, saying, "No, Keith! Not like this!"

ZouZou said that she received menacing phone calls telling her to "keep her mouth shut" and she eventually fled London for her native France to hide herself. But even as late as 1995 she was still getting threatening calls.

Her opinion was that the builders were the hired thugs who carried out the murder, but that the idea that this was over some money dispute was false. "It was a much higher hand which dealt the deal," she related. She thought the gangster Tom Keylock organized the killing. Brian Jones was a big problem because he was the creator and owner of the Rolling Stones name.[287]

---

[285] Wohlin, pp. 148-150

[286] Email from Roxanne Fontana, 4/21/25

[287] Who Killed Brian Jones? Musical Genius and Quintessential Rolling Stone by gomerevibz@steemit

In 2013 a sensational story broke in the *Daily Mail*, just after the Stones returned to play Hyde Park, where they'd given a tribute concert to Brian 44 years before. It alleged that on the very morning of his death, Keith went out to Cotchford and drew a knife on him during a heated argument over the rights to the band's name. Jan Bell, the daughter of Frank Thorogood, went to the Sussex police and they filed a formal report.

"She said that her father had told her a number of years ago that on the day of Brian's death, Messrs Mick JAGGER and Keith RICHARDS visited Brian JONES at the farm in the morning and her father was present when Brian was asked by both men whether he would give up the name of the "Rolling Stones" to them and agree to a financial settlement."

"Brian apparently declined to do so and it is alleged that THOROGOOD calmed them down and both JAGGER and RICHARDS left the house."

The police officer who interviewed Jan Bell then made arrangents to meet with Jagger's and Richards' lawyers to discuss this specific incident. But his Assistant Chief Constable intervened and prevented this meeting from ever happening.[288]

---

[288] Keith Richards 'drew a knife on Brian Jones hours before he died': As the Rolling Stones play Hyde Park again, a new twist in the riddle of the guitarist's death in swimming pool by Scott Jones, Daily Mail 7/6/13

Evidently this incident was hearsay from the Thorogood family grapevine. It was further embellished in 2020 by some comments from sister-in-law Laurie Bell, who added, "Brian looked at Frank as a father figure and a best friend... he never wanted Frank to leave, to the point of offering Frank money to stay. Brian was in a terrible state when they threw him out of the band..."

"Went to my brother's [Jan's husband] before the [Covid] lockdown, he was telling me the two blokes who went to confront Brian about naming rights was Keith and a henchman... Frank was there and had to get between them to break it up... according to my brother, Mick was not there."[289]

The Stones had apparently been rehearsing at Olympic through the wee hours on the morning in question,[290] making it unlikely that Keith and a henchman [Keylock?] went out to Cotchford thereafter to confront Jones. Frank Thorogood had perhaps heard about- or even witnessed- the June 8th knife incident and in his later years jumbledly passed it on to family members as first-hand information. And tried to present himself to them as the unsung hero. Yet the most disturbing feature of Jan Bell's story is that police shut down any further inquiry.

It behooves the Thorogood family to clear Frank's name, if that were even possible, since he has been a convenient scapegoat in the multilayered nest of lies surrounding this crime. But his participation is undeniable: the injured wrist, the Durophet tablets, the burn pile, the attack on Joan Fitzsimmons. His integrity would have been salvaged, by this point, in this internet age, a decade after Bell's revelations. What is more likely is that the Thorogood family knows how horrifically enmeshed Frank was in the Brian Jones murder.

Further, they could shed some light on any role his nephew Danny may have played. Danny Thorogood initially lodged together with Frank when they worked at the Redlands estate, but he wasn't mentioned in any accounts from Cotchford. Yet judging from this funeral photo, he seems to have admitted either being there at the time of Jones' death, or had admitted something just as pertinent.

---

[289] Crimewatch 1994 comments section@ youtube
[290] Trynka, p. 330

Sometime in the afternoon of July 2nd, Tom Keylock had driven from Cotchford to Redlands to pick up Keith Richards.[291] He subsequently took him to Olympic Studios in London. And Keylock would later claim that he was forced to return to Redlands to retrieve a guitar that Keith forgot—and for years used this as an alibi that he was not at Cotchford when Jones died. An alibi that could have been corroborated only by Keith Richards.

And music writer Keith Altham helped cover for Keylock and Richards. In the 2012 documentary *The Second Wave*, in footage from the 90s, Altham claims Keylock appeared at Olympic "about two o'clock in the morning" to inform the Stones of Brian's death.[292] Yet for Paul Trynka's 2014 biography he pushes this back to "about midnight, or one o'clock", which Trynka uses to ridicule the idea that Keylock was involved in the murder.[293] Altham was conveniently unaware that Sussex police had taken note of a man fitting Keylock's description to a tee in the kitchen at Cotchford at 12:30 AM; and that Ian Stewart, upon receiving a call at Olympic from Keylock's wife, was the one who informed the Stones entourage at approximately 1:10 AM.

---

[291] Rawlings, p. 126
[292] The Second Wave@youtube 54:25
[293] Trynka, p. 334

The question we have to ask is: Was Keith in any way complicit in Brian's murder? Because if Allen Klein decided it was time for Brian Jones to die, using Keylock to sway the builders and quash the police investigation

wasn't quite enough. Klein needed another inside man to protect Keylock- and therefore himself- from incrimination. There was no better choice than Richards- overloaded with drugs and the occult, who had connived for years to remove Jones from the Stones.

And the answer is: only as a prop. Only as an unwitting accessory. Richards didn't recall that Keylock did any work for him at all on the night Brian died.[294] And as he pieced Cotchford together over the following years, Keith openly wondered where the hell Keylock was at the time.[295] His alibi didn't surface until the 90s, and there is no indication that Richards was ever even informed of supposedly forgetting his guitar.

His penchant for brutal honesty showed his suspicions and divulged some inside information to *Rolling Stone* magazine in 1971: "Someone called us up at midnight and said, 'Brian's dead'. Well, what the fuck's going on? We had these chauffeurs working for us and we tried to find out… Some of them had a weird hold on Brian…"

"…We were completely shocked. I got straight into it and wanted to know who was there and couldn't find out. The only cat I could ask was the one I think who got rid of everybody and did the whole disappearing trick so that when the cops arrived, it was just an accident. Maybe it was. Maybe the cat just wanted to get everyone out of the way so it wasn't all names involved, etc. Maybe he did the right thing, but I don't know."

"I don't even know who was there that night and finding out is impossible… It's the same feeling with who killed Kennedy. You can't get to the bottom of it."

---

[294] Rawlings, p. 146
[295] Email from Roxanne Fontana, 4/21/25

Brian contacted ZouZou shortly after the three Stones visited him at Cotchford. "Brian was in really bad bad shape and he was begging to see me and he wanted to talk to me," she related. "It was about three weeks before he died. He told me he asked Mick to help him, to take him to a hospital because he knew he was really going- he didn't say die- that he was going to die. But he knew that he was in such a bad shape that he couldn't go on like this. And Mick just told him to fuck off. Keith too."[296]

About two weeks before he died Marianne Faithfull threw six coins to get a reading from the I Ching about Brian Jones. She was with Mick Jagger in their London apartment. It came up: Death by water. "My God! Do it again!" Jagger insisted and again it came up: Death by water. Jagger was so concerned he tracked Jones down and located him at the Redlands estate. There is no indication Richards was there at the time.[297]

After an argument after dinner, Jones lunged at Jagger with a knife and missed stabbing him by inches. A fistfight ensued and Jones ran outside and jumped into the Saxon moat. Jagger jumped in after him and dunked his head again and again into the muddy water.[298]

---

[296] Brian Jones: Life and Death of a Rolling Stone by Danny Garcia
[297] Faithfull, pp. 169-170
[298] Wecht, p. 149

That spring Brian was reportedly in his best mental health in a year as he'd gotten off the recreational drugs, faded away from the Stones and was beginning plans to form his own supergroup. And word of these intentions leaked, through Keylock, back to Allen Klein. "Will someone tell me why we are paying that little shit all of that money?!" he raged. "And he's still making trouble?!"[299]

Alexia Korner warned him that even talking about such a supergroup could be dangerous. It would be a threat to both the Stones and the Beatles and it could cost the wrong people a lot of money.[300] One planned band member was John Lennon, who had recorded a track with Jones at Apple Studios as a group they had saucily pen-named The Balls. Another member would be Jimi Hendrix.

Jones also rehearsed with Steve Winwood, Steve Marriot, Mitch Mitchell, John Mayall, Mickey Waller and Denny Lane. Korner said Brian once played 14 hours straight- all his own material.[301] Jones was aware that some of his demos had been stolen and Anna Wohlin did in fact witness Frank Thorogood going through them.[302]

Is it any wonder that Jones' creative legacy was also murdered? Tapes would be proof not only of his virtuosity, and rapport with other accomplished musicians. It is not out of the question that his estate, with proof of his original compositions, could have sued Messrs Jagger and Richards for songwriting royalties. Instead, any surviving tapes were tossed onto the burn pile along with his personal and legal papers.

Yet there were reservations. He wouldn't play guitar in front of Alexis Korner, preferring to freestyle on saxophone or other instruments. He was drinking excessively and "on those asthma inhalers all the time… He wasn't in a good state." And for John Mayall he did manage some guitar, but "his hands and brain simply weren't matching up… very wobbly. Not really in the condition to be putting something together."[303]

There was evident damage from his drug excesses- even with glimpses of recovery- and Brian thereby was perfect fodder for the character

---

[299] Rawlings, p. 117
[300] Fitzgerald, pp. 232-234
[301] Rawlings, pp. 103-105; Fitzgerald, p. 17
[302] Wecht, p. 154
[303] Trynka, pp. 309-310

assassination which followed his bodily assassination. "They did everything to create headlines which said, 'Drink and drugs are bad'. If you look back at the social and political times in '68, '69, to work out why did the police- or why did the Home Office- or why did the government want to spin the death of Brian Jones- you have to look at the growth of the counterculture- the growth of drugs for the first time as a social problem," Scott Jones observed.

"And you have to look at what the Home Office were advising the government. They were basically saying, 'Get rid of the pop stars and you get rid of the drug problem.' If you then look at the busts that were carried out on Brian- on Mick in particular- on Brian especially- all of those drug busts- 90% of them actually involve the police trying to plant drugs inside the Stones' property. The politics of the time was to say, 'We're going to destroy these bands. We're going to destroy this counterculture that's emerging'."

"And people like Brian Jones represented it more than anyone else. Again, if you go back to the Stones in '67, '68, '69- Mick and Keith were not quite as rebellious as Brian. They certainly weren't connected to drink and drugs as Brian. They didn't look as counterculture as Brian."

"He was the one. He was the DNA of the band's rebellious nature. And when he died, he became a poster boy. The government could literally hold him up and say, 'This is what happens to you kids if you take drugs.' And it was a total, total misuse of actually what had happened."

"The man had been killed. But rather than get to the truth, they would rather spin out a lie, to suit their own political agenda about what was going on in their minds with society and the emerging counterculture at the time."

"Because the truth was Brian Jones was killed. The truth is Brian Jones didn't die of drink and drugs."[304]

---

[304] Brian Jones: Life and Death of a Rolling Stone by Danny Garcia

But the real truth was even deeper than Scott Jones was willing to fathom. This was a political crime, to be sure- dovetailing with the assassinations so prevalent in America in the 60s. But there was something even more sinister to this one than silencing another liberal icon. This was a Satanic sacrifice that delved into heroin and the occult, which had fueled murderous jealousies within the Rolling Stones. And this was a hit by organized crime, which had seeped into the fabric of the popular music industry. Specifically Jewish organized crime- which could control the police, the coroner, the press, the Home Office, and every moneyed fiber of society. Allen Klein regarded Brian Jones as nothing more than just another disposable goy.

At 10:00 AM on the morning of July 3rd the Stones filed into the BBC's Lime Grove Studios to film their new single *Honky Tonk Women* for *Top of the Pops*. They mimed their performance, excepting Jagger and Watts, and Mick Taylor used one of Brian's Firebird guitars, looking quite depressed. Jagger gave an energetic dance routine and that evening attended a garden party hosted by his future financial advisor, Prince Rupert Loewenstein. Mick wore the white tunic he would unveil two days later at Hyde Park as he schmoozed with the likes of Princess Margaret and Lord Tavistock, amid sixty complaints to the police about noise.[305]

Anna Wohlin stayed at the Londonderry Hotel in the company of Astrid Lundström.[306] She did not attend the free concert, which drew half a million people. She confided to her that nobody seemed to take the drowning seriously enough. She was sure Brian was still alive when he was fished from the pool since she could feel his pulse.[307]

"Why didn't you help Brian?! Why did you leave him in the pool?!" she shouted at Thorogood. *"It's your fault! I hate you!"*

Frank was as cold as ice. He didn't show any sympathy and I noticed that he'd stopped shaking. He didn't respond to my accusations either.

Janet came running towards us when Frank and I turned Brian on to his front to try to get the water out of his lungs. She said that the telephone was out of order.

---

[305] Rawlings, p. 168; Wyman, pp. 529-530
[306] Wohlin, p. 209
[307] Wyman, p. 528

Frank stood up and started walking towards the house. Janet, whom I later discovered was a trained nurse, helped me to lay Brian flat on his back, and sank down on her knees and started heart massage while I tried to give Brian the kiss of life.

"Why didn't you help Brian?!" I sobbed. "Why didn't you pull him out instead of calling for me?! How the hell could you leave him there?! What's wrong with you?! And where were you when it happened?!"[308]

On July 5th the new Rolling Stones lineup made their first public appearance at Hyde Park. They played a 50-minute set that was out of tune and sounded atrocious. Mick entreated the crowd to "cool it and listen" as he prepared them for an excerpt from Percy Bysshe Shelley, from *Adonais*, selected in advance by Marianne Faithfull. "Cool it for a minute, because I would like to say a few words about what I feel about Brian, and I'm sure you do... and what we feel about him just going when we didn't expect

---

[308] Wohlin, p. 195

him to." He then recited the poetry in a "clumsy, heartless and awkward manner,"[309] piping away like somebody reading a weather forecast.[310]

Peace, peace! He is not dead, he doth not sleep-
He has awakened from the dream of life-
'Tis we, who lost in stormy visions, keep
With phantoms an unprofitable strife
And in mad trance, strike with our spirit's knife
Invulnerable nothings- We decay

Like corpses in a charnel; fear and grief
Convulse us and consume us day by day
And cold hopes swarm like worms within our
living clay.

The One remains, the many change and pass;
Heaven's light forever shines, Earth's shadows fly;
Life, like a dome of many-colored glass,
Stains the white radiance of Eternity,
Until Death tramples it to fragments.- Die,
If thou wouldst be that which thou seeks!

Later that summer Mick quietly bought the Rolling Stones name from Brian's parents.

---

[309] Landis, p. 168
[310] Fitzgerald, p. 249

FOURTEEN

JULY 2, 1969

We have reached the point where we can assimilate what we have learned thus far, and can re-establish what occurred on the night of Brian Jones' murder. This is still an ongoing investigation, 55 years after the fact.

There remain 60 or more critical pages from the initial police investigation that have never seen the light of day, due to the 75-year rule of the Crown Protection Service. These include reports from Cotchford and interviews with Joan Fitzsimmons and Michael Ziyadeh. Additionally, the "Klein Report", which Sam Cutler discussed in great detail with Allen Klein, has never surfaced and is probably locked away in an ABKCO vault in Manhattan.

The Thorogood family is withholding information that is damning not only to Frank, but likely to his nephew Danny. And the same can be said as regards the families of Morris Tucker and Johnny Betsworth. And also the relatives of Tom and Frank Keylock, and even Janet Lawson. This is an opportunity for an enterprising young journalist who lives in Great Britain and can track down these relations.

Because as of this writing, their family names are stained with the blood of a good man.

Brian Jones was not a saint; he had serious character flaws. But he was a fundamentally good man, whose genius helped transform the cultural landscape of the 60s- so eggshell fragile after the sudden and horrific assassination of the U.S. president. It was a timeframe that still brings enormous impact to the current age.

Allen Klein has been exposed as a murderer and he built his empire on the blood of Sam Cooke and Brian Jones. There may be others. Their heirs need to go after ABKCO, Inc., to recover what rightfully belongs to these musical geniuses. Murder renders every last one of Klein's contracts with these artists null and void – and this pertains to the entire Sam Cooke catalogue and the Rolling Stones from 1963-1971. It stinks to high heaven that a negotiator would own, in entirety, the creative work of a recording artist.

The surviving Stones are another potential source for adding truth to this investigation. Possibly they can speak more freely, knowing that Klein was the godfather who ordered Brian's murder. Apparently they were hoodwinked by him early on. Sam Cutler stated they were called into his office and told about what had actually happened, that he had it investigated. But Klein told them, "There was nothing they could do about it, because it was too big for them to fight."[311]

Allen Klein, in other words, portrayed himself as fighting against the same establishment that had decided to make an example of Brian Jones, who'd been a casualty of the counterculture war, as sure as Kennedy was

[311] http://samcutler.tumblr.com

a casualty of the Cold War. And he'd even hired private detectives to find out the "facts". This uncanny ability to lie to people's faces may trace back to his years in the Hebrew Orphanage.

[Note: Who were Klein's private detectives?]

Besides murdering the man, Allen Klein put salacious effort into murdering Brian Jones' legacy – ransacking his antiques collection, burning his exotic wardrobe, destroying any trace of musical creativity. Brian had been one of the spearheads – on a par with Bob Dylan and John Lennon – forging rock 'n roll's cultural explosion, in which a rebellious generation shaped their identity. Jones' classical musicianship and multi-instrumental talents gave the Stones a melodic flair which rivaled the Beatles, and has disappeared from their songbook since his death. It is obvious that he was gypped out of songwriting credits on numerous hits. Hopefully a more equitable distribution for his children – Simon, Belinda, Mark, Julian, John and Barbara – can be sorted out when ABKCO is rightfully sued for back royalties.

In the latter part of the morning Jones made a trip to the Stones offices in London. His purpose was financial and there is a reasonable chance he met with Allen Klein. Brian was seeking to ensure that Rolling Stones Ltd. made a final payment to the builders at his estate. Klein was seeking to ensure that Brian Jones got murdered, which was why he'd made a special trip to the English capitol. Jones, according to Wyman, was chauffered back to Cotchford in a car hired by the office.

Tom Keylock, in the meantime, left his mistress Janet Lawson behind at Cotchford and drove down to the Redlands estate. Anita Pallenberg, seven months pregnant, was there along with Keith Richards. At some point that afternoon Keylock and Richards made the 90-minute trip to Olympic Studios in London for that night's rehearsal. Keylock would return to Cotchford sometime before 9:00 PM, but wouldn't admit it for 40 years- instead claiming that he'd gone back to Redlands for one of Keith's guitars.

Early that afternoon Jones and one of his builders ran into Nicholas Fitzgerald and his companion at the Hay Waggon pub, a mile from the estate. Jones got a lift home from them and they spent the remainder of the afternoon relaxing by the pool.

Later that afternoon in the garage apartment Lawson saw Frank Thorogood prepare a batch of hash cakes and spike a steak & kidney pie with an unknown drug. That drug was likely Durophet, which degraded upon baking and left an amphetamine-like residue in Jones' urine, and had no causal connection to his death. Yet the coroner, Angus Sommerville, had the audacity to misleadingly pronounce Jones' death as due to "drowning whilst under the influence of alcohol and drugs." And he may have omitted the shattering discovery of algae in the lungs.

At approximately 5:00 PM Suki Potier arrived at Cotchford with three unknown girlfriends. Michael Ziyadeh, Gary Leeds and Jackie Shaw were also on the grounds at the estate. Joan Fitzsimmons arrived in her cab at 9:00 PM sharp to pick up Ziyadeh and the rest of the small party were chased away then by Tom Keylock.

In the meantime Fitzgerald and his companion had been sent on a wild goose chase to Hayward Heaths, 12 miles away, to pick up a girl who never showed up. The carpet-fitters David Gibson and Eddie Loakes were working in the music room and were the last to leave. They were asked to do so by Keylock. As they picked up their gear Jones apparently pleaded with them to spend the night, telling them he was terrified for his life.

Joan Fitzsimmons' mother said that her daughter "left the house about a half hour before Brian Jones was drowned," thereby placing the murder about 9:30 PM. She would have learned this from Joan, who was informed by Thorogood, who had called about 6:00 AM and confessed to the killing. So this is Thorogood's time estimate, made under duress. But given that sunset on July 2nd in tht area is about 9:20 PM, and twilight extends to almost ten, it is more likely that Brian was killed closer to 10:00 PM.

This makes sense when we consider that when Fitzgerald and his companion returned to the Cotchford estate, they were blinded by a set of headlights from a vacated foreign car, with its driver's door left open. Its purpose there was to ward off any potential intruders, and there is a possibility its driver was Danny Thorogood.

The floodlights that they had seen being installed that afternoon very likely were part of the ruse to ensure that Jones was in the pool area as darkness fell. They were on at the time of the murder and Brian was likely consulted about their placement. This would also be a good excuse to get him into his swim trunks.

Anna Wohlin was initially present but went upstairs to take a telephone call. And Lawson was somewhere in the house, maybe in the music room as she claimed.

That left Jones alone outside with Thorogood, Keylock, Tucker and Betsworth. He had a young Afghan hound and a cocker spaniel who remained inside.

The builders made a coordinated attack and essentially gang-tackled Jones and carried him to an animal trough near the pool. During the scuffle, apparently, is when Thorogood injured his wrist. Brian may have managed to cry out for help. Fitzgerald said he witnessed three of them holding his body upside-down in the trough. And- based upon the available information- Les Hallett was alerted by the distress and was an earwitness to what occurred. His is an independent corroboration.

Once Brian's body went limp they carried it over to the pool and shoved it into the deep end. Lawson was roused from the house and saw him at the bottom; she was the blonde girl screaming in Fitzgerald's 1983 police statement. He saw Lawson and Keylock at one side of the pool, and Thorogood, Tucker and Betsworth at the other- their faces blotched by the bright floodlights. The car in the drive screeched away and Keylock noticed Fitzgerald and went up to the summer house to confront him.

Anna Wohlin rushed outside to find "Frank and the nurse were standing by the pool, Brian was there and they were doing nothing at all. [She] dove in and tried to fish him out" as Wohlin explained in a phone call to Jim Carter-Fae later that night. Her police report also stated she dove in and got him off the bottom. And that as they applied artificial respiration, "I felt Brian's hand grip mine."

MURDER

Allen Klein
Tom Keylock
Frank Thorogood
Morris Tucker
Johnny Betsworth

<u>ACCESSORY AFTER THE FACT</u>

Janet Lawson
Danny Thorogood
Dr. Angus Sommerville
Frank Keylock
Sussex police superintendent R.M. Hipgrave
Detective Sergeant Peter Hunter
Detective Chief Inspector Robert Marshall
Chief Constable T.C. Williams
Drugs officer Mickey Dann

AFTERWORD

I had another dream about Brian Jones while I was in the middle of this project, and it made me feel I was on the right path.

It was a summer's day and I was sitting on a picnic blanket in the grass, near a grove of trees, about fifty yards away from the smouldering aftermath of a campfire. A group of people were standing around it, swaying to a beat led by Mick Jagger, who was chanting out an a capella version of *Sympathy for the Devil*. He was wearing a headband and Apache-style clothing and this was his first-ever rendition of the song.

When he was finished he walked past me with a couple members of his entourage and I said admirably, "Nice poetry." He didn't reply but I could tell by the look in his eyes he was very pleased with himself.

I got up and was instantaneously transported to Brian Jones' grave. He stood there in his mop of blonde hair in a dark suitcoat and white pants. He extended a firm hand and we humbly shook hands and I knew I had a true friend.

* * * * *

A special thanks goes out to Roxanne Fontana, who obtained an early copy of this book and apprised me of a significant error. She was a godsend. Her clutch expertise saved me a bit of embarrassment and, more importantly, sharpened the discernment of the gospel truth. Brian Jones deserves no less.

BIBLIOGRAPHY

The True Adventures of the Rolling Stones by Stanley Booth, Chicago Review Press, Chicago (2000)

Faithfull: An Autobiography by Marianne Faithfull with David Dalton, Cooper Square Press, New York (1994)

Brian Jones: The Inside Story of the Original Rolling Stone by Nicholas Fitzgerald, G.P. Putnam's Sons, New York (1985)

Allen Klein: The Man Who Bailed Out the Beatles, Made the Stones, and Transformed Rock 'n Roll by Fred Goodman, Houghton Mifflin Harcourt, New York (2015)

Golden Stone: The Untold Life and Tragic Death of Brian Jone by Laura Jackson, St. Martin's Press, New York (1992)

Anger: The Unauthorized Biography of Kenneth Anger by Bill Landis, HarperCollins, New York (1995)

The Final Truth: Who Killed Christopher Robin? by Terry Rawlings - 2015. Sam Cooke: The Truth by B.G. Rhule (2022)

Brian Jones: The Making of the Rolling Stones by Paul Trynka, Plume, New York (2015)

Up and Down with the Rolling Stones by Tony Sanchez, Wm. Morrow, New York (1979)

Mick Jagger: Everybody's Lucifer by Tony Scaduto, David McKay Company, Inc., New York (1974)

The Early Stones by Terry Southern, Hyperion Press, Westport, CT (1992)

From Crimescene to Courtroom by Cyril Wecht and Dawna Kauffmann, Prometheus Books, Amherst, NY (2011)

She's a Rainbow: The Extraordinary Life of Anita Pallenberg by Simon Wells, Omnibus Press, London (2020)

The Murder of Brian Jones; The Secret Story of My Love Affair with the Murdered Rolling Stone by Anna Wohlin with Christine Lindsjöö, Blake Publishing Ltd., London (1999)

Stone Alone: The Story of a Rock 'n Roll Band by Bill Wyman with Ray Coleman, Da Capo Press, Boston (1990)

Rolling with the Stones by Bill Wyman, DK ADULT, London (2002)

PHOTO CREDITS

COVER Gered Mankowitz PREFACE Mark and Colleen Hayward//
Redferns ONE Savills; Jim Gray//Keystone//Getty; Daily Mail; Evening
Standard//Getty; Taylor Humphries//Getty; Bentley Archive//Popperfoto//
Getty TWO John Downing//Getty; Savills; Helen Spittal; John Downing//
Getty; John Downing//Getty THREE Wikimapia; Chichester Post;
Terry Rawlings; Terry Rawlings; Terry Rawlings FOUR Savills; Terry
Rawlings; Rolling Stones; Helen Spittal; Daily Mail FIVE Daily Mirror;
The Sun; Daily Mail; Jenny Barnes; Stephen McKay; John Downing//
Getty; Trinity Mirror//Alamy SIX Vas Karageoris//Rolling Stones
Archive; Trevor Humphries; The Brian Jones Resource; John Downing//
Getty; John Downing//Getty SEVEN Crazymama.blogspot; Daily Mail;
Evening Standard//Getty; Daily Mirror//Getty EIGHT J. Wilds//Getty;
Gered Mankowitz; Andy Boulton//Keystone//Getty; Daily Mirror//Getty;
Stern; tumblr; Michael Cooper; Evening Standard NINE Chester Kessler;
Marjorie Cameron; Church of Satan; Fred Mott//Evening Standard//
Getty; Jean Pierre Bonnotte; Pinterest; Jeff Barker TEN garyrocks.files.
wordpress.com; BBC; notfadeawaygallery.com; Getty; Pinterest; Michael
Ward//Getty; Bill Wyman; Steve Hoffman; Pinterest; Larry Liu; Ethan
Russell; Alamy; Brian Jones Fan Club; Brian Jones Fan Club ELEVEN
Richard Carlin; Performance Magazine; Salem-News.com; Pinterest; Daily
Mirror TWELVE RCA Victor; B.G. Rhule; L.A. Times; LAPD; Ernest
C. Withers//Panopticon Gallery; Getty; Getty; B.G. Rhule; B.G. Rhule;
B.G. Rhule THIRTEEN Vogue International Industries; Michael Joseph;
Getty; Jean Pagliuso; nickelinthemachine.com; Brian Jones Friends and
Fans; Chris Walter//Wire Image; Getty FOURTEEN Brian Jones Friends
and Fans; Brian Jones Friends and Fans; bellaonline.com BACK COVER
Laurie McGowan

www.ingramcontent.com/pod-product-compliance
Lightning Source LLC
Chambersburg PA
CBHW051311120626
46547CB00015B/2194